BIKES

A ROAD RACING SUPERBIKE.   PRICE : $ 430.00 PLUS.

BIKES

A How-to-do-it Guide to Selection, Care, Repair, Maintenance, Decoration, Safety, and Fun on your Bicycle

by STEPHEN C. HENKEL
Illustrated by the Author

THE CHATHAM PRESS, INC.
RIVERSIDE, CONNECTICUT
DISTRIBUTED BY THE VIKING PRESS, INC.

SBN: 85699-033-7

Library of Congress Catalog Card Number: 73-171354
Manufactured in the United States of America

ACKNOWLEDGMENTS

The original idea for this book came from Christopher Harris of The Chatham Press. To Chris, his associate John Hinshaw, and their assistant Christine O'Shea, I am particularly indebted.

Help with facts and information on bikes came from many quarters. I wish especially to thank for their help, interest, suggestions, and encouragement: Mr. Jim Hayes of the Bicycle Institute of America; Mr. Ernest Gilman of the Bianco and Gilman Bike Shop in Darien, Connecticut; the people at Haden's Bike and Hobby Shop in Harwichport, Massachusetts; Mr. Peter Kaszonyi of the Schwinn Bicycle Company; Mr. William B. Laighton, Jr. of the Columbia Manufacturing Company, Inc.; Mr. E. J. McVoy of the Murray Ohio Manufacturing Company; Mr. Michael Botwinick and his staff at the Metropolitan Museum of Art in New York City; and Mrs. Lois Keeler of the Darien Public Library staff. Many useful suggestions resulted from manuscript reading by John Hoy, Jeb Henn, David Constant, John Canaan, and Bill Lohrer. My thanks also go to Mrs. Ella Westphal, who patiently read and typed my practically indecipherable handwritten manuscript, and corrected syntax and spelling in a most efficient manner.

To my wife, Carol, who took the kids out for bike rides on many a dreary Saturday afternoon so I could concentrate on manuscript and pictures, and to my sons Charlie, five, and Laird, two, I offer my deepest appreciation for their forebearance during the preparation of this book.

— Stephen C. Henkel
Darien, Connecticut

CONTENTS

TO CHARLIE AND LAIRD

PREFACE

The United States is in the midst of a Great Bicycle Renaissance. As this book was written, eight and a half million bikes were expected to be sold in 1971—a pretty high figure considering that ten million cars were expected to be sold in the same period! And it's not just one age group that's buying. People of all ages are climbing aboard bicycles. A few years ago nine out of every ten bikes were pedalled by youths from five to fourteen years old. But in 1971, three out of every ten were sold for adult use.

Whether you're a new rider, an old rider, or just a would-be rider, if you're looking for useful information but don't want to get bogged down in too many details, this book is written for you. You will find out why you might want to choose a three-speed bike instead of a ten-speed—or even a one-speed—bike. You will learn the secrets of cadence, clinchers, derailleurs, and rattraps. You will get the inside story on proper lubrication and repairs—and much more. If you don't know anything about bikes, this book will give you a proper start on the road to bicycling fun. If you know a little, there is a good chance you will learn something more. And if you already know everything there is to know about bikes, or can't read yet, perhaps you will get a kick out of the pictures.

In any case, Pedal Power is the cry today. And this book is designed to give you Extra Pedal Power, and help you get the most fun and use out of your bicycle. So read it—and happy pedalling!

FIGURE 1-1: DRAISINE, 1816

FIGURE 1-3: LADIES' HOBBY HORSE, 1819

FIGURE 1-2: GENTLEMEN'S HOBBY HORSE, 1818

FIGURE 1-4: MACMILLAN'S BICYCLE - 1840

FIGURE I-5: BONESHAKER, 1868

1

BIKE STYLES:
Today and Yesterday

According to Webster's definition, a bicycle is "a vehicle with two wheels tandem, a steering handle, a saddle seat, and pedals by which it is propelled." If it has three wheels or one, it's not a bicycle. If the wheels are side by side instead of fore and aft, it's not a bicycle. If it has no pedals, or is propelled by a motor, technically, it's not a bicycle.

BIKES THROUGH HISTORY

The origin of the bicycle has caused much controversy. Who invented such a contraption in the first place? Bicycle-like machines were in existence before 1800, although none met the dictionary definition above. The earliest known picture of something resembling a bicycle can be seen in a stained glass window in a church in Stokes Pages, England, and is dated 1642. But nobody knows if the machine pictured was real or just a figment of the artist's imagination—or even if it had two wheels. Around 1690 a Frenchman, the Comte de Sivrac, is reported to have invented a two-wheeled vehicle called a "walk-along." The rider propelled it by sitting on a saddle and pushing the ground with his feet. A variety of such machines were in use by the late 1700's.

Another early ancestor of the bicycle was conceived in 1816 by Baron Karl von Drais, a game warden in Karlsruhe, Germany. Called the "Draisine," it was an all-wood affair which differed from earlier walk-alongs in one important way: the front wheel pivoted, enabling the rider to steer his machine. In 1818 and 1819, Dennis Johnson of London designed and began manufacturing

FIGURE 1-6: PENNY FARTHING, 1870

FIGURE 1-7: OLDREIVE'S TRICYCLE

FIGURE 1-8: SINGER'S XTRAORDINARY, 1879

two distinct versions of this, one for men and one for women. The difference was the inclusion of a horizontal bar on the men's style but not on the ladies'. This basic distinction between men's and ladies' bikes remains unchanged after more than a century and a half. Bikes like Johnson's were variously known as "swift-walkers," "hobbyhorses," "dandy horses," "celeripeds," "velocipedes," "patent accelerators," "bivectors," "bicipedes," and "pedestrian curricles."

The design of bike-like machines improved steadily after these initial inventions. In 1840, Kirkpatrick MacMillan of Scotland added reciprocating cranks to the front of his version of the hobbyhorse. They were similar to pedals and were connected to the rear wheel by rods. On the basis that MacMillan was the first to meet today's dictionary definition of a bicycle, he is often described as the true inventor of the bike.

In 1861, the first bike using rotary cranks attached to the front hub was invented by a couple of French brothers named Michaux. It ran on wooden wheels with iron tires and came to be known as the "boneshaker," since the ride tended to be quite rough. In 1868, solid rubber tires replaced the iron ones, making the ride somewhat more comfortable.

In 1870, the "penny farthing," also called the "high-wheeler" or "ordinary," emerged in England. As this developed, the front wheel tended to get bigger and bigger, supposedly for more speed. By the 1880's, front wheels of 50 inches in diameter (in contrast to rear wheels of about 17 inches) were common. Such ma-

FIGURE 1-9: STARLEY'S ROVER, 1885

chines were normally heavy, weighing 50 to 75 pounds, although you could buy an ordinary that weighed 150 pounds, or one that weighed only 21 pounds. Carrying the big-wheel idea to an extreme, a man named Old-reive came up with a huge-wheeled bike (actually a tricycle) where the rider sat *inside the wheel* to pedal.

During the same period, there was a counter-movement in design which tended toward smaller front wheels and placement of the seat further back, giving the rider a more secure position. Singer's "Xtraordinary," also known as a "dwarf safety velocopede," is an example of this variety. In 1885, an Englishman named J. K. Starley brought out his "Rover," an early prototype of the bicycle of today. In 1888, L. B. Dunlop, an Irish veterinary surgeon, came forth with the pneumatic or air-filled tire. By the 1890's, the bicycle had matured. The typical design, called a "safety" bicycle, had come to look much like today's, with two 28-inch wheels, a chain drive, and pneumatic tires.

CURRENT STYLES

The most common bicycle seen in the recent past has been the so-called "touring model" or "English racer" (which often isn't either English or a racer). This bike has flat handlebars, a well-padded seat, and fenders. Plenty of touring-model bikes are still being sold, but some new departures in design have taken hold in the 1960's and early 1970's. One fad is typified by the "automotive-theme" bike, which can vary from the common "high-rise" variety to quite exotic styles. A

FIGURE 1-10:
1890'S SAFETY
BICYCLE

12

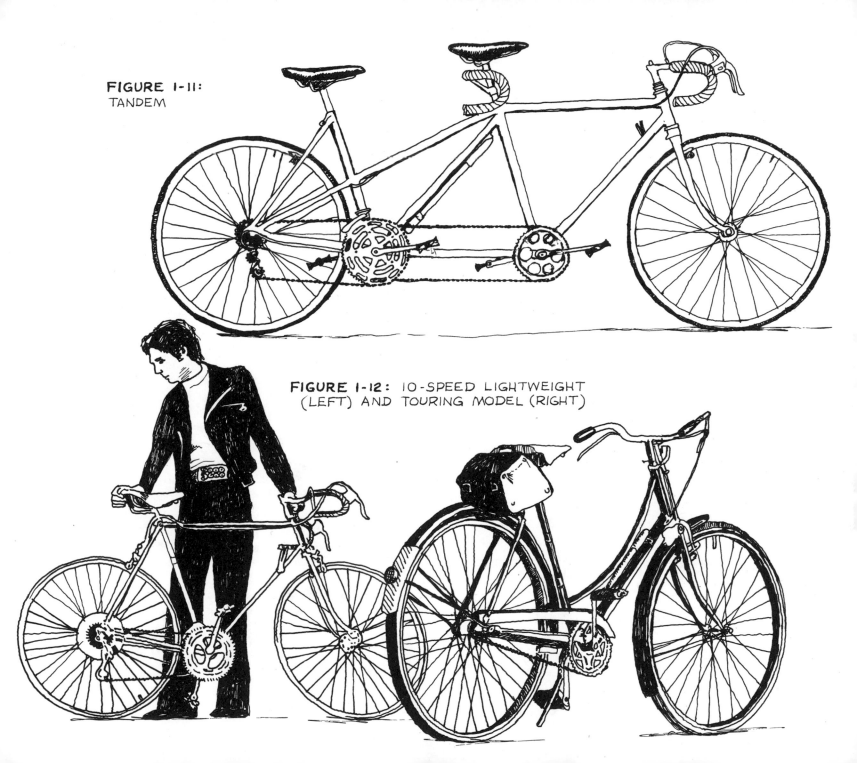

FIGURE 1-11: TANDEM

FIGURE 1-12: 10-SPEED LIGHTWEIGHT (LEFT) AND TOURING MODEL (RIGHT)

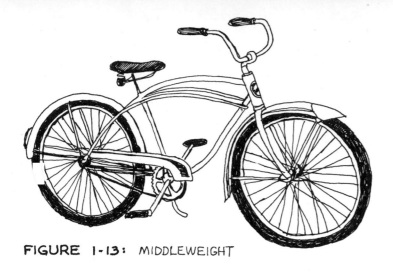

FIGURE 1-13: MIDDLEWEIGHT

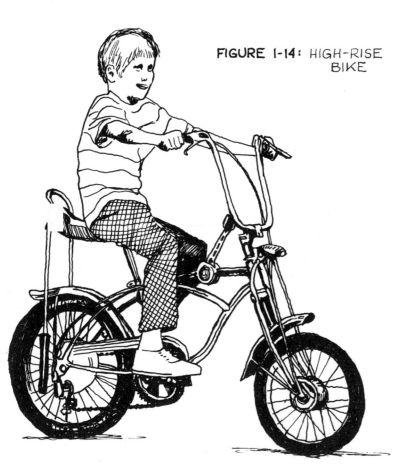

FIGURE 1-14: HIGH-RISE BIKE

manufacturer's catalogue describes one such model as being "available with gears, full-floating ride, stick shift, numbered lever, five speeds forward, bucket seat, buffed rear 'slick' tire, shock-absorbing saddle struts, front aluminum brake drum, shock-absorbing front fork...." If the bike also includes a V-8 engine and dual exhaust, the catalogue doesn't mention it.

The first high-rise bicycle was built in the early 1960's by a group of Southern California teenagers who saw the fun in selecting individual parts and letting their imaginations run wild. They worked out the basic idea of combining small wheels with high-rising handlebars and an elongated seat. The style was then "discovered" by the major American bicycle companies in 1963.

Another variety is the 10- or 15-speed lightweight bicycle. It has turned-down handlebars, a small, hard seat, no fenders, and is equipped with a "derailleur" (pronounced "day-rye-err" in French but also acceptably translated into English as "de-rail-er") gear-shifting mechanism. How this works is explained in Chapter 2. A derailleur's main advantage is that it allows a wider variety of gear ratios than other types of gears, and thus makes it easier to pedal, particularly up and down hills.

Other currently fashionable bikes, and some non-bikes, deserve mention here. These are:

The middleweight bike. It has an extra-sturdy frame and balloon tires. It is generally intended for heavy-duty, rough use such as delivering newspapers. But because of its weight and wide tires, it is somewhat harder to pedal than other bikes, especially when pumping uphill.

The two-passenger tandem bike. For years known as a "bicycle built for two," this machine rides two people sitting one behind the other, both pedalling in unison. The front handlebars control the steering;

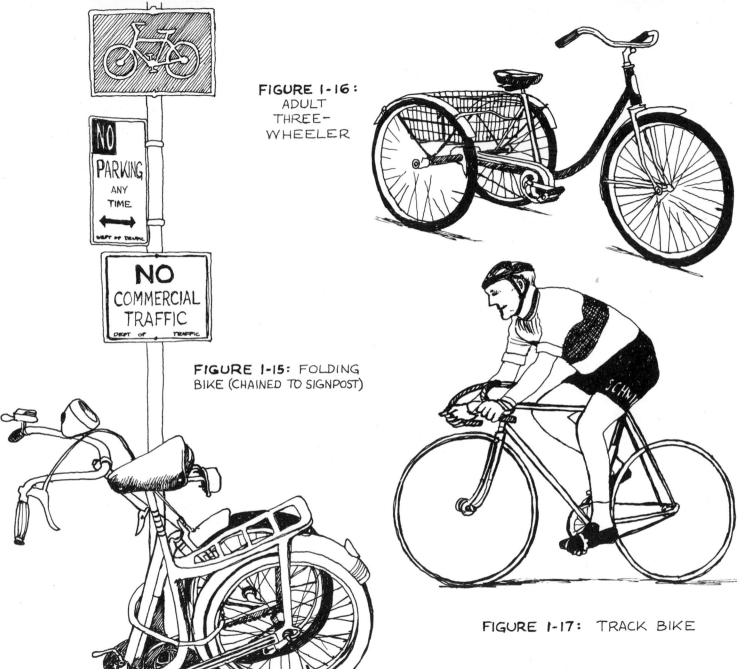

FIGURE 1-16: ADULT THREE-WHEELER

FIGURE 1-15: FOLDING BIKE (CHAINED TO SIGNPOST)

FIGURE 1-17: TRACK BIKE

15

the rear handlebars are fixed. Unless each rider pumps his own weight, this bike can be hard on the stronger rider who has to compensate. But it's terrific for togetherness!

The folding bike. This design has a hinge so that the bike can fold over on itself, making it smaller for storage and carrying. Usually the handlebars and seat post are also designed to telescope into the frame to further shrink the folded mechanism.

The unicycle. This has only one wheel and so, by definition, it is a "non-bike." The pedals are mounted on its one wheel and the contraption has no handlebars. You steer by leaning in the direction you want to go. It is not very practical, partly because it is difficult to balance and partly because its top speed is limited since the pedal cranks cannot be geared down. However, unicycles are fun to try! To learn, find a level space with a wall or fence you can lean against to steady yourself. (A narrow alleyway where you can touch both walls is ideal.) Or balance yourself with the aid of two poles. Stopping can be tricky, though—the pedals are attached directly to the hub, and so a unicycle can have no brakes. To stop or slow down, you must slow the pedals.

The adult three-wheeler. This is also a "non-bike" because it has three wheels. It is mainly used as a vehicle for the elderly or infirm who are unable to balance a regular bike. But it, too, can be a fun bike to ride.

The track bike. The ultimate in lightweight bikes, these cut off poundage by eliminating everything unnecessary, including brakes. They typically weigh 18 to 20 pounds and are strictly for track racing. They have special wheels with fewer spokes and lightweight track tires, are ungeared, and utilize an extra-high pedal-to-wheel ratio for sustained high speeds on level surfaces.

FIGURE 1-18: UNICYCLE

BICYCLE WORLD RECORDS

A number of world records have been established by bicycle enthusiasts; nearly all utilize bikes of unusual design or style. According to the *1971 Guinness Book of World Records,* some of these are:

The longest bike. Built in England in 1968, it was 35 feet, 4 inches long and carried 20 passengers. It had over 100 feet of chain, and weighed 1000 pounds—empty.

The tallest bike. The tallest bicycle-like machine was a 32-foot tall unicycle, ridden by Steve McPeak in Seattle, Washington, in 1969. In 1968, McPeak rode a 13-foot unicycle 2000 miles from Chicago to Las Vegas in six weeks. The tallest true bike may still be the "Eiffel Tower Tandem" built in 1896, which was 20 feet high.

The fastest bike. The world's fastest bike was ridden at 127 miles per hour by José Meiffret on the Frieburg, West Germany, race track on July 19, 1962, using a racing car as a windbreaker. The bike had a huge chainwheel and a tiny rear sprocket, giving a gear ratio number of 275. Figure 1-23 shows an earlier record holder. That bike went a mere 108.92 m.p.h. and had a gear ratio number of 252.

Greatest distance in an hour. The record for the greatest distance covered on a bike in one hour was 76 miles, 604 yards, set by Leon Vanderstuft on a race track in France on September 30, 1928.

The slowest bike. Tsugunobu Mitsuishi of Tokyo, Japan, rode the slowest bike in the world—he sat on it without moving for 5 hours, 25 minutes in 1965.

FIGURE 1-22: A LONG BIKE. THIS IS A MERE 8-SEATER. THE RECORD HOLDER WAS A 20-SEATER, 35 FEET 4 INCHES LONG.

FIGURE 1-19 : ARTICULATED TANDEM

Parade bikes. These are the really off-b[...]
traptions such as the bikes you see clowns rid[...]
circus, or local bicyclists pedalling in your tow[...]
day parades. Generally they're fun to experim[...]
but are not very practical for everyday use. E)[...]
the unicycle, now available as a commercial [...]
most parade bikes are custom-built by their o[...]
creative bike shops. They can be designed in [...]
of crazy styles.

FIGURE 1-20 : EXTREME AUTOMOTIVE STYLE

FIGURE 1-21 : SUPER H[...]

FIGURE 1-23:
A FAST BIKE

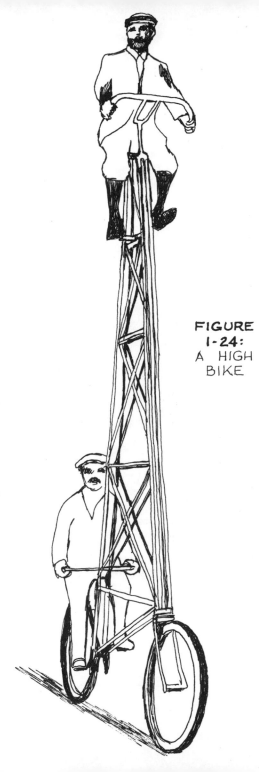

FIGURE
1-24:
A HIGH
BIKE

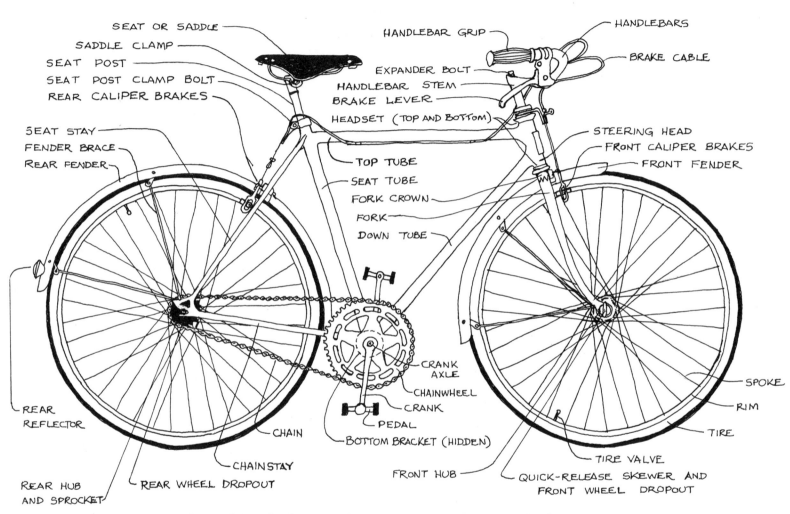

SEAT OR SADDLE

SADDLE CLAMP

SEAT POST

SEAT POST CLAMP BOLT

REAR CALIPER BRAKES

SEAT STAY

FENDER BRACE

REAR FENDER

HANDLEBAR GRIP

HANDLEBARS

BRAKE CABLE

EXPANDER BOLT

HANDLEBAR STEM

BRAKE LEVER

HEADSET (TOP AND BOTTOM)

STEERING HEAD

FRONT CALIPER BRAKES

FRONT FENDER

TOP TUBE

SEAT TUBE

FORK CROWN

FORK

DOWN TUBE

REAR REFLECTOR

CHAIN

CHAINSTAY

REAR WHEEL DROPOUT

REAR HUB AND SPROCKET

CRANK AXLE

CHAINWHEEL

CRANK

PEDAL

BOTTOM BRACKET (HIDDEN)

FRONT HUB

QUICK-RELEASE SKEWER AND FRONT WHEEL DROPOUT

TIRE VALVE

SPOKE

RIM

TIRE

FIGURE 2-1: NAMES OF BIKE PARTS

20

2

THE ANATOMY OF A BIKE

Getting to the practical side of modern bicycling (which is what this book is mostly about), let's look first at the anatomy of a bike. Figures 2-1 and 2-2 show typical bikes with all the major parts named. You should be at least vaguely familiar with these parts in order to understand the pages that follow.

BASIC COMPONENTS

One way to examine a bike's anatomy is to look at its various component parts. Basically, all parts of a bike fit into nine categories: frames, saddles, handlebars, pedals, gears, brakes, wheels, tires, and accessories. The first eight of these are discussed in this section. Accessories are described separately because there are so many of them.

Frames. Designs of frames differ in minor respects from manufacturer to manufacturer, and vary in size and style within each manufacturer's stock. One main variation is found in the number of "top tubes" used. The top tube is the horizontal bar from the steering head to the seat tube on men's bikes; frames may have one (for lightness) or several of them (for strength). Major variations also occur in frame size, weight, and overall strength. As for size, the rule is: the taller the rider, the larger the frame. Usually lightweight frames, which require somewhat less pedalling effort than the heavier frames, are also proportionately less strong. However, the lightweight frames of high quality racing bikes are made of special alloys and have reinforced joints which improve strength to a level comparable

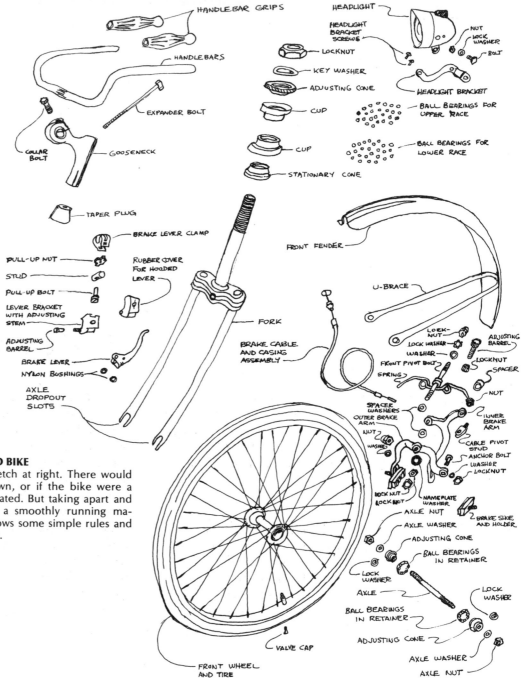

HANDLEBAR GRIPS

HEADLIGHT

HEADLIGHT BRACKET SCREWS

NUT

LOCK WASHER

BOLT

HANDLEBARS

LOCKNUT

KEY WASHER

ADJUSTING CONE

HEADLIGHT BRACKET

EXPANDER BOLT

CUP

BALL BEARINGS FOR UPPER RACE

COLLAR BOLT

GOOSENECK

CUP

BALL BEARINGS FOR LOWER RACE

STATIONARY CONE

TAPER PLUG

FRONT FENDER

BRAKE LEVER CLAMP

PULL-UP NUT

RUBBER COVER FOR HOODED LEVER

U-BRACE

STUD

PULL-UP BOLT

LOCK-NUT

LEVER BRACKET WITH ADJUSTING STEM

FORK

BRAKE CABLE AND CASING ASSEMBLY

LOCK WASHER

WASHER

ADJUSTING BARREL

ADJUSTING BARREL

FRONT PIVOT BOLT

LOCKNUT

SPACER

SPRING

BRAKE LEVER

NYLON BUSHINGS

NUT

AXLE DROPOUT SLOTS

SPACER WASHERS

INNER BRAKE ARM

OUTER BRAKE ARM

CABLE PIVOT STUD

NUT

WASHER

ANCHOR BOLT

WASHER

LOCKNUT

LOCK NUT

LOCK NUT

NAMEPLATE WASHER

AXLE NUT

BRAKE SHOE AND HOLDER

AXLE WASHER

ADJUSTING CONE

BALL BEARINGS IN RETAINER

LOCK WASHER

AXLE

LOCK WASHER

BALL BEARINGS IN RETAINER

ADJUSTING CONE

VALVE CAP

AXLE WASHER

FRONT WHEEL AND TIRE ASSEMBLY

AXLE NUT

Figure 2-2: EXPLODED VIEW OF A ONE-SPEED BIKE

There are 127 separate bike pieces in the sketch at right. There would be a lot more if extra accessories were shown, or if the bike were a 3-speed or 10-speed model. It looks complicated. But taking apart and reassembling all these bits and pieces into a smoothly running machine is not difficult for the novice if he follows some simple rules and procedures. Chapters 6 and 7 tell how to do it.

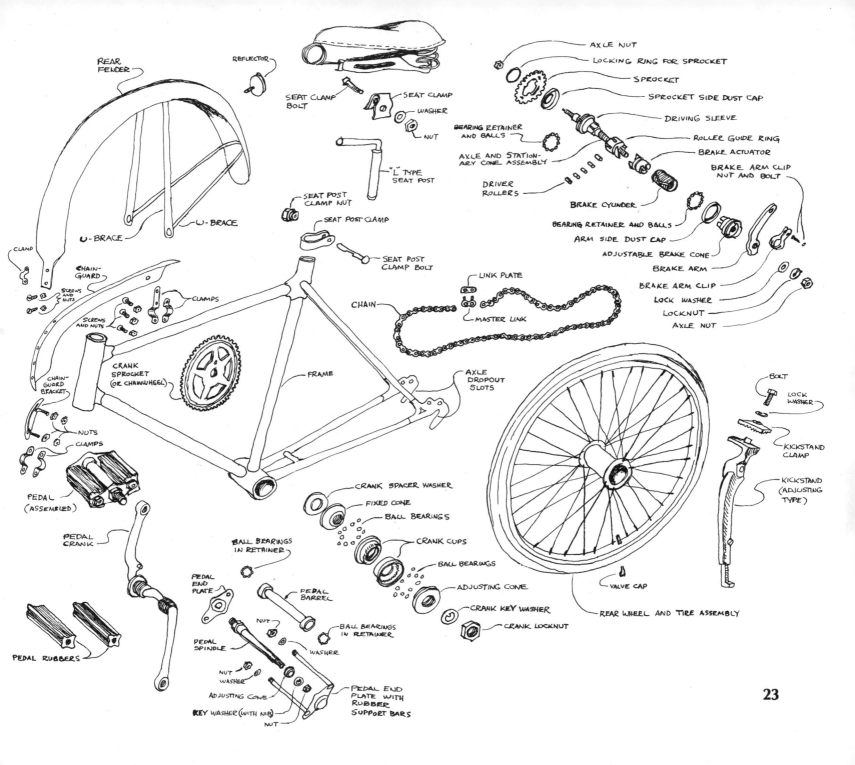

REAR FENDER

REFLECTOR

SEAT CLAMP BOLT

SEAT CLAMP

WASHER

NUT

"L" TYPE SEAT POST

AXLE NUT

LOCKING RING FOR SPROCKET

SPROCKET

SPROCKET SIDE DUST CAP

DRIVING SLEEVE

BEARING RETAINER AND BALLS

ROLLER GUIDE RING

BRAKE ACTUATOR

AXLE AND STATIONARY CONE ASSEMBLY

BRAKE ARM CLIP NUT AND BOLT

DRIVER ROLLERS

BRAKE CYLINDER

BEARING RETAINER AND BALLS

ARM SIDE DUST CAP

ADJUSTABLE BRAKE CONE

BRAKE ARM

BRAKE ARM CLIP

LOCK WASHER

LOCKNUT

AXLE NUT

U-BRACE

U-BRACE

CLAMP

CHAIN-GUARD

SCREWS AND NUTS

CLAMPS

SCREWS AND NUTS

SEAT POST CLAMP NUT

SEAT POST CLAMP

SEAT POST CLAMP BOLT

LINK PLATE

CHAIN

MASTER LINK

CHAIN-GUARD BRACKET

CLAMPS

CRANK SPROCKET (OR CHAINWHEEL)

FRAME

AXLE DROPOUT SLOTS

BOLT

LOCK WASHER

NUTS

CLAMPS

PEDAL (ASSEMBLED)

PEDAL CRANK

CRANK SPACER WASHER

FIXED CONE

BALL BEARINGS

CRANK CUPS

BALL BEARINGS

ADJUSTING CONE

CRANK KEY WASHER

CRANK LOCKNUT

KICKSTAND CLAMP

KICKSTAND (ADJUSTING TYPE)

BALL BEARINGS IN RETAINER

PEDAL END PLATE

PEDAL BARREL

PEDAL SPINDLE

NUT

BALL BEARINGS IN RETAINER

WASHER

NUT WASHER

ADJUSTING CONE

KEY WASHER (WITH NIB)

NUT

PEDAL END PLATE WITH RUBBER SUPPORT BARS

PEDAL RUBBERS

VALVE CAP

REAR WHEEL AND TIRE ASSEMBLY

23

with heavier frames. Some variation may by found in the size of the angles at the joints of different frames, but this variation is of minor importance to the average bicyclist.

Saddles. Saddles generally fall into three categories: banana or "solo polo" saddles for high-rise bikes; "touring" saddles; and "racing" saddles. The novice rider usually prefers the banana type or the touring type because they are softer and are often considered more comfortable than the narrower racing saddle.

However, the enthusiast who considers bicycling a sport to be taken seriously often opts for a racing saddle. You can't beat it for efficiency because it positions the rider forward, putting more of his weight on the handlebars and pedals. Because it is narrow, it interferes less with thigh movement and, because it is hard, it absorbs less of the rider's energy, giving him more to transmit to the pedals. Once the bicyclist becomes accustomed to the hunched-over, forward position used with a racing saddle, he usually finds this type at least as comfortable as any of the others.

If you get a new bike and your thighs are sore or chafed during the first few days of riding, it is probably not the seat. Stick with it for a couple of weeks and see if you get used to it. Both you and the seat may need a little "breaking in."

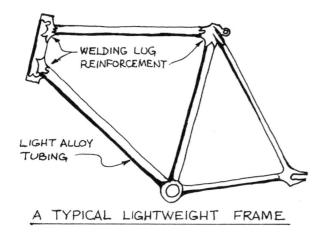

A TYPICAL LIGHTWEIGHT FRAME

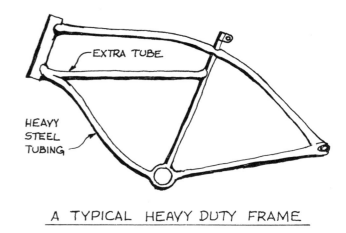

A TYPICAL HEAVY DUTY FRAME

FIGURE 2-3: FRAME TYPES

Note also that some seats are adjustable forward and backward as well as up and down; others aren't.

Handlebars. "Bars" also come in three basic styles: flat or "upright" (traditionally the most common); "turned-down" used mostly on derailleur-equipped lightweight bikes and racing machines); and "high-rise" (used on some pre-teen and teenage bikes). With upright handlebars, the rider sits up straight. Turned-down handlebars are normally used along with a racing saddle and the bent-over or crouched position. While the crouched position may look uncomfortable relative to sitting up, experts swear by it. They say it is more effective because it cuts down wind resistance, and you can use more muscles for a longer time with your back arched slightly; it's better for the health of your back; it is easier to breathe in this position; and, somewhat surprisingly, they say it's more comfortable than the sitting-up position because your body weight is more evenly distributed between the saddle and handlebars.

High-rise handlebars are designed mainly for style rather than comfort or efficiency, and are not generally used on adult machines. If they are raised to the point where the rider is forced to ride with his hands at chin height, they can make steering difficult and riding hazardous. Thus, if high-rise bars are used, they should

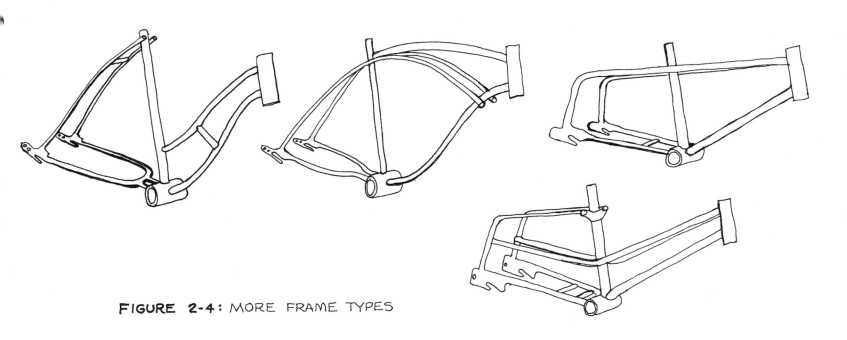

FIGURE 2-4: MORE FRAME TYPES

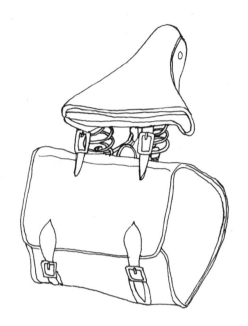

EUROPEAN-STYLE
"MATTRESS SADDLE"
FOR TOURING BIKES.
(NOTE TOURING BAG
STRAPPED TO BACK.

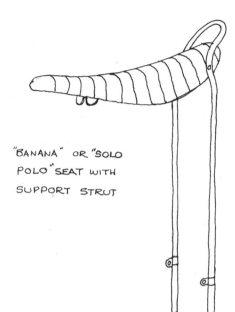

"BANANA" OR "SOLO
POLO" SEAT WITH
SUPPORT STRUT

FIGURE 2-5:
SADDLE TYPES

RACING SADDLES

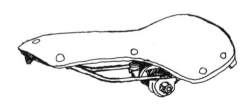

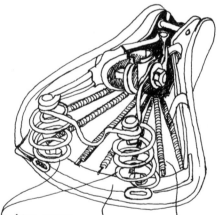

EUROPEAN
STYLE —
BOTTOM
VIEW

TWO SHOCK
ABSORBING
SPRINGS HELP
SMOOTH BUMPY
RIDES.

ONE HALF
INCH RUBBER
PADDING

COIL
SPRINGS
GIVE
MATTRESS-
LIKE
SUPPORT

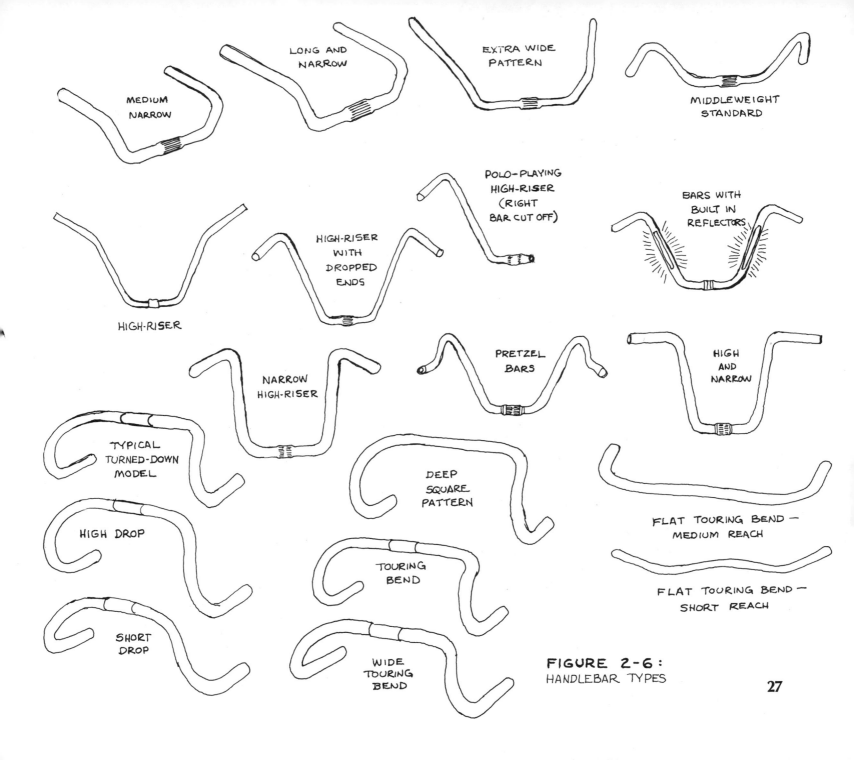

MEDIUM NARROW

LONG AND NARROW

EXTRA WIDE PATTERN

MIDDLEWEIGHT STANDARD

HIGH-RISER

HIGH-RISER WITH DROPPED ENDS

POLO-PLAYING HIGH-RISER (RIGHT BAR CUT OFF)

BARS WITH BUILT IN REFLECTORS

NARROW HIGH-RISER

PRETZEL BARS

HIGH AND NARROW

TYPICAL TURNED-DOWN MODEL

DEEP SQUARE PATTERN

HIGH DROP

FLAT TOURING BEND — MEDIUM REACH

SHORT DROP

TOURING BEND

FLAT TOURING BEND — SHORT REACH

WIDE TOURING BEND

FIGURE 2-6:
HANDLEBAR TYPES

27

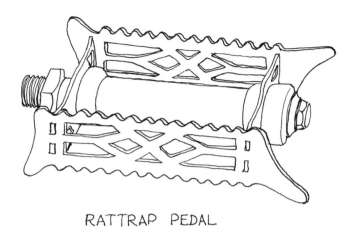

RATTRAP PEDAL

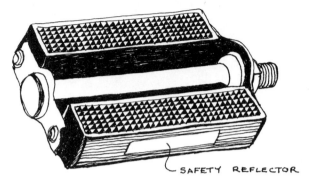

SAFETY REFLECTOR

RUBBER TREAD PEDAL

FIGURE 2-7: PEDAL STYLES

be adjusted so that the rider reaches down (to about waist level) rather than upward.

Pedals. These can be either the usual "hard rubber" variety, or the specialized "rattrap" type used on racing bikes, which are lighter and provide more grip to the rider. But rubber pedals are less expensive and are standard equipment on most non-racing bikes. (Some rubber pedals come with reflectors attached to the front and back—a neat safety idea.)

Gears. There are two types of gears used today: "epicyclic" and "derailleur." Epicyclic gears are operated by a lever on the handlebars or frame, or by foot action on the pedals, and are contained within the rear hub; they are commonly available in two- and three-speed mechanisms.

The derailleur gear-shifting mechanism utilizes clusters of different-sized sprockets to produce varied

Figure 2-8: HOW A DERAILLEUR MECHANISM WORKS
The picture opposite shows how a derailleur mechanism works. When the *rear derailleur speed control lever* is moved forward from the position shown, the *rear derailleur* begins moving out sideways (away from the bike). As the derailleur moves sideways, it pulls the *chain* with it. As the chain moves to the side, it "derails" off of one sprocket in the *rear sprocket cluster* and onto the next sprocket. The spring-loaded *tension roller* keeps the chain taut but "gives" as the chain rises off the teeth of one sprocket and onto another. The *jockey roller* keeps the chain feeding smoothly onto the rear sprocket cluster, and keeps the S shape in the chain so the tension roller can do its job. The *front derailleur*, operated by the *front derailleur speed control lever*, works exactly the same as the rear derailleur, but doesn't have a tension roller, since only one is needed to keep the entire loop of chain taut.

Since the derailleur works by literally shoving the chain from one sprocket to another, proper rider technique is needed to make the operation easy and smooth, and to avoid damage to the mechanism. The chain must be in motion, feeding into the sprocket, for the derailleur to do its job. But the rider, while pedalling, should not be applying any real power; to do so might damage the derailleur. And the control levers should be moved gently and smoothly for most effective operation.

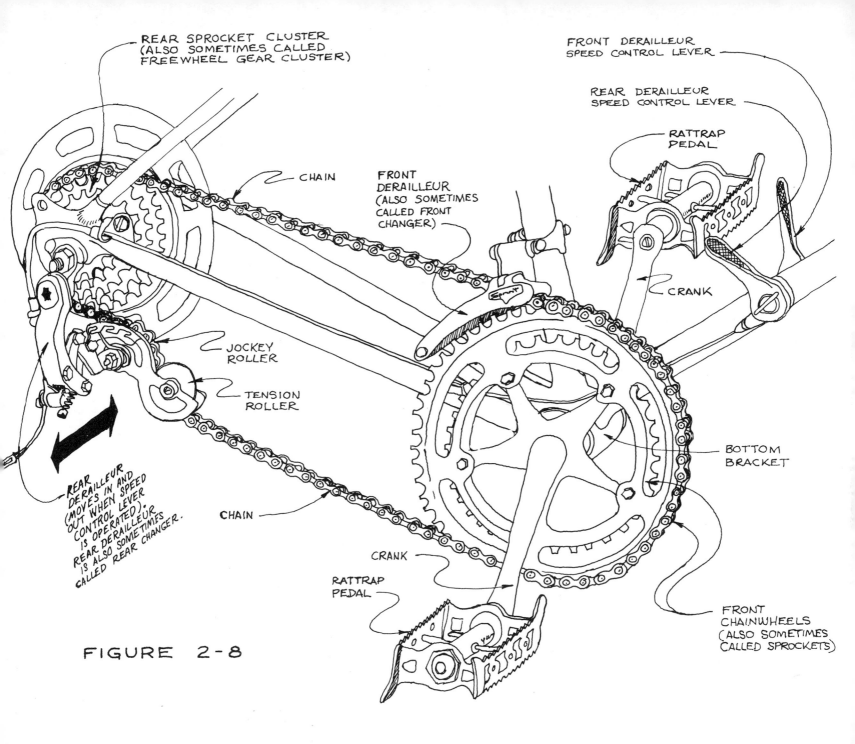

REAR SPROCKET CLUSTER
(ALSO SOMETIMES CALLED
FREEWHEEL GEAR CLUSTER)

FRONT DERAILLEUR
SPEED CONTROL LEVER

REAR DERAILLEUR
SPEED CONTROL LEVER

RATTRAP
PEDAL

CHAIN

FRONT
DERAILLEUR
(ALSO SOMETIMES
CALLED FRONT
CHANGER)

CRANK

JOCKEY
ROLLER

TENSION
ROLLER

BOTTOM
BRACKET

REAR
DERAILLEUR
(MOVES IN AND
OUT WHEN SPEED
CONTROL LEVER
IS OPERATED).
REAR DERAILLEUR
IS ALSO SOMETIMES
CALLED REAR CHANGER.

CHAIN

CRANK

RATTRAP
PEDAL

FRONT
CHAINWHEELS
(ALSO SOMETIMES
CALLED SPROCKETS)

FIGURE 2-8

Figure 2-9: SHIFTING DERAILLEUR GEARS
Here and on the facing page are shown the different ways the chain is arranged for each of the ten speeds on a ten-speed bike. Note the position of the control levers for each of the speeds. Also note the way the tension roller changes position to keep the chain tight regardless of which combination of sprockets is being used. This page shows the combinations using the small chainwheel. The facing page shows the big chainwheel combinations.

MEDIUM LOW (FOURTH) GEAR. GR = 50.
GENERAL PURPOSE CHAIN POSITION.

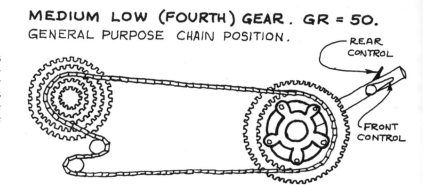

BOTTOM LOW (FIRST) GEAR. GR = 33.
FOR VERY STEEP HILL CLIMBING. BECAUSE OF THE LOW GEAR RATIO, IT'S EASY TO START UP IN THIS GEAR.

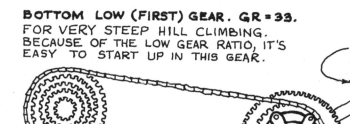

MEDIUM (SIXTH) GEAR. GR = 62.
GENERAL PURPOSE CHAIN POSITION.

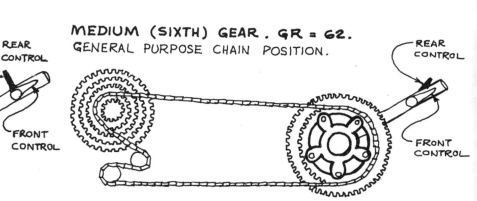

VERY LOW (SECOND) GEAR. GR = 40.
FOR STEEP HILL CLIMBING.

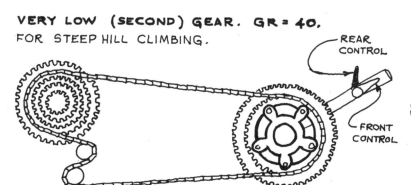

HIGH (EIGHTH) GEAR. GR = 75.
FOR ABOVE AVERAGE CRUISING SPEED.

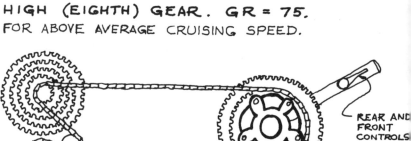

LOW (THIRD) GEAR. GR = 44.
FOR MODERATE HILL CLIMBING.

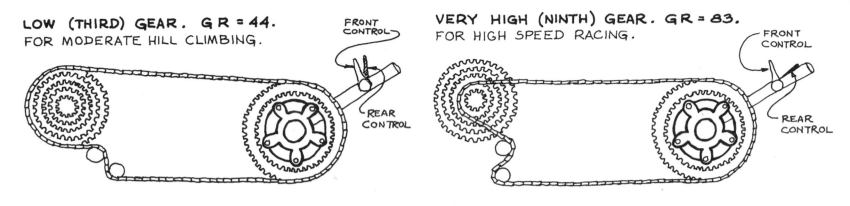

VERY HIGH (NINTH) GEAR. GR = 83.
FOR HIGH SPEED RACING.

MEDIUM (FIFTH) GEAR. GR = 54.
GENERAL PURPOSE CHAIN POSITION.

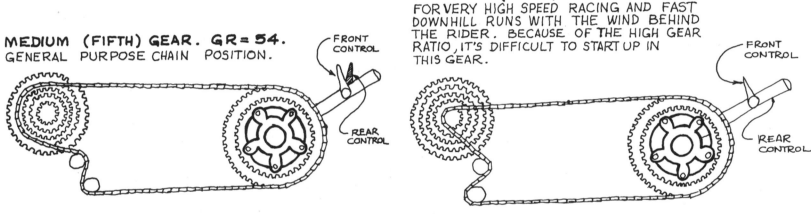

TOP HIGH (TENTH) GEAR. GR = 100.
FOR VERY HIGH SPEED RACING AND FAST DOWNHILL RUNS WITH THE WIND BEHIND THE RIDER. BECAUSE OF THE HIGH GEAR RATIO, IT'S DIFFICULT TO START UP IN THIS GEAR.

MEDIUM HIGH (SEVENTH) GEAR. GR = 67.
FOR ABOVE AVERAGE CRUISING SPEED.

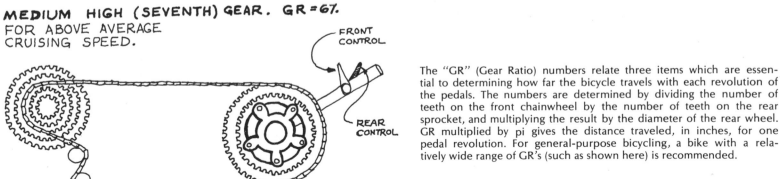

The "GR" (Gear Ratio) numbers relate three items which are essential to determining how far the bicycle travels with each revolution of the pedals. The numbers are determined by dividing the number of teeth on the front chainwheel by the number of teeth on the rear sprocket, and multiplying the result by the diameter of the rear wheel. GR multiplied by pi gives the distance traveled, in inches, for one pedal revolution. For general-purpose bicycling, a bike with a relatively wide range of GR's (such as shown here) is recommended.

31

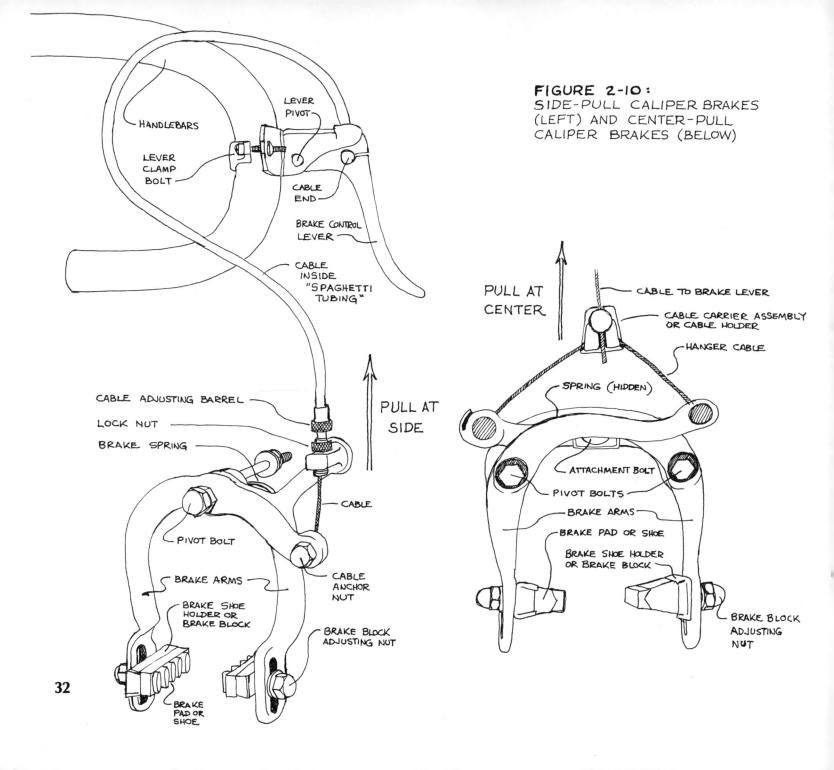

HANDLEBARS

LEVER
PIVOT

LEVER
CLAMP
BOLT

CABLE
END

BRAKE CONTROL
LEVER

CABLE
INSIDE
"SPAGHETTI
TUBING"

CABLE ADJUSTING BARREL

LOCK NUT

BRAKE SPRING

PULL AT
SIDE

CABLE

PIVOT BOLT

BRAKE ARMS

CABLE
ANCHOR
NUT

BRAKE SHOE
HOLDER OR
BRAKE BLOCK

BRAKE BLOCK
ADJUSTING NUT

BRAKE
PAD OR
SHOE

FIGURE 2-10:
SIDE-PULL CALIPER BRAKES
(LEFT) AND CENTER-PULL
CALIPER BRAKES (BELOW)

PULL AT
CENTER

CABLE TO BRAKE LEVER

CABLE CARRIER ASSEMBLY
OR CABLE HOLDER

HANGER CABLE

SPRING (HIDDEN)

ATTACHMENT BOLT

PIVOT BOLTS

BRAKE ARMS

BRAKE PAD OR SHOE

BRAKE SHOE HOLDER
OR BRAKE BLOCK

BRAKE BLOCK
ADJUSTING
NUT

32

pedal-to-rear-wheel speed ratios. ("Sprockets" are the toothed wheels at the pedals and rear wheel, on which the chain rides.) The derailleur consists of a moveable cage or "chainguide" which surrounds the bicycle's chain close to the point where it meshes with the sprocket clusters. When an actuating lever is pulled, the derailleur pushes against the side of the chain, literally "derailling" it from one sprocket to another of a different size. (Figure 2-8 shows this action in detail.)

Derailleurs will give up to 15 different speeds. By combining epicyclic and derailleur gears on a bike, it is possible to reach 24, 36, or more speeds, but most people will settle for somewhere between one and 15 speeds, and that's the range most readily available. A chart in the Appendix shows the principal types of gears with their advantages and disadvantages.

Brakes. Four different types of brakes are available: "coaster," "side-pull caliper," "center-pull caliper," and "drum" brakes. The coaster brake is contained inside the rear wheel hub of almost all non-geared (one-speed) bikes, and some epicyclic-geared bikes. When the bike is back-pedalled, a brake sleeve or set of brake disks is squeezed against the moving hub, stopping the wheel.

Both center-pull and side-pull caliper brakes (see Figure 2-10) utilize small rubber pads squeezed against the rim of the wheel (either front, back, or both) to stop the bike. The pads are controlled by a hand lever located on the handlebars. Center-pull caliper brakes are thought by some to apply a more uniform stopping pressure since the mechanism is symmetrical on both sides of the wheel rim, but this is by no means a proven fact. Side-pull brakes, though not physically symmetrical, do squeeze evenly on the wheel rim if properly adjusted and lubricated. So, if good maintenance proce-

dures are followed with both types of brakes, no significant difference in stopping power is noticeable.

Drum brakes are much the same as those used on motorcycles and automobiles, and are a specialty item. They are usually found only on tandems, which need heavy-duty stopping power because of the extra weight, or for looks on automotive-theme high-risers. As on cars, the mechanism involves brake shoes inside a hollow metal drum. When the shoes are actuated, they push outward against the rim of the drum, rubbing against it and stopping it.

Wheels. Wheels vary as to diameter, number of spokes, and type of rim. Diameters (measured to the *outside* edge of the tire) range from 12 inches to 28 inches, depending on the size and style of bike. The standard adult and teen-age sizes are 26 or 27 inches—with the exception of the high-rise models which have smaller wheels, generally 20 inches, or sometimes 20 inches in back and 16 inches in front.

Larger wheels have the advantages of slower turning, easier pedalling, and a higher top speed. Smaller wheels are suitable for children's bikes, increase maneuverability somewhat, and contribute to the style of high-rise models.

One general design of spokes and rim is standard for most bikes and doesn't vary much. However, ultra-lightweight racers use lighter rims and fewer spokes to permit somewhat easier pedalling and a faster ride. On the other hand, light rims are more prone to damage from common road hazards than are the heavier standard ones.

Tires. Tires generally come in three types: the popular "clinchers," between 1¼ inches and 1¾ inches in width; "balloon clinchers," between 2 and 2¼ inches; and the "sewn type" used for racing, between ¾ inch

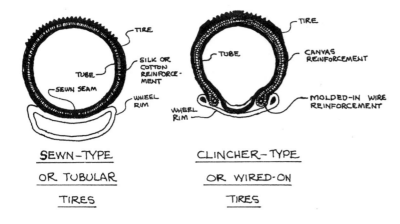

SEWN-TYPE
OR TUBULAR
TIRES

CLINCHER-TYPE
OR WIRED-ON
TIRES

FIGURE 2-11: TIRE TYPES

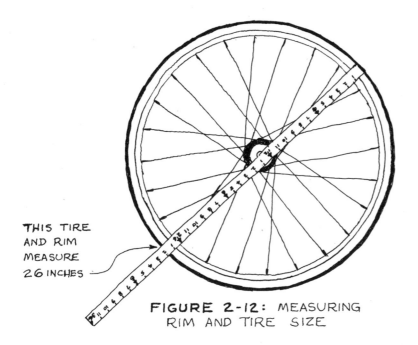

THIS TIRE
AND RIM
MEASURE
26 INCHES

FIGURE 2-12: MEASURING
RIM AND TIRE SIZE

and 1¼ inches. Standard clincher tires (also called "wired-ons") are specifically intended for rough use on the typical wide range of road surfaces encountered by the touring bicyclist, and are standard equipment on most bikes other than high-rise or racing models. Balloon tires are usually used today only on small bikes for young children, on special-purpose bikes such as tandems or other heavy load carriers, or on style-setters such as some high-risers. Sewn tires are strictly for the racing buff and come in a variety of styles. These tires, designed for ultra-lightness and low friction, are rather easily punctured and are not recommended unless maximum speed or endurance is of the highest priority to the rider.

ACCESSORIES

You can get many different kinds of accessories for bikes; most require minimum instruction for installation and use. The pictures on these pages show some of the different gadgets available. A list of the most popular ones and their uses appears in the Appendix. It includes 41 different items, and if you installed one of each on your bike, you might have trouble getting the bike going because of all the weight—which brings me to my first point about accessories.

The best way to get top speed out of your bike, assuming it has been well cared for and is in good mechanical condition, is to *keep it light*. This means not adding accessories, but taking them off. Some you'll need for safety if not for comfort and convenience, but if your objective is maximum speed, I would not encourage you to add a radio, bulky baskets and saddle bags, speedometer, generator set, or other items that are heavy or draw power from the wheels. In the entire list, there are really only three accessories that can be added which actually improve speed: toe clips and straps, cleated bike shoes, and rattrap pedals. All these things weigh very little and make it easier to apply power on the upstroke of the pedal as well as the downstroke—a technique called "ankling" which we'll discuss later.

Of course, the idea of stripping a bike to keep it ultra-lightweight can be overdone. Saving a few ounces here and there is reasonable if you are a racing enthusiast entering regular competitions. But for around-town riding, you would never notice the difference in top speed or pedal effort required to lug an extra pound or two. So, if you want speed, keep your bike light but don't sacrifice too much comfort or convenience (and certainly not safety) for a few extra hundredths of a mile per hour. In the words of my local bike dealer: "What are you going to do, ride it or carry it?"

A few of the accessories deserve special mention for one reason or another.

Locks. Bike locks come in four basic kinds: built-in locks; long-shank padlocks; chain locks; and cable locks. None of these is always effective. Even if you carefully lock your bike before leaving it, it could be gone when you return. How? The thief simply lifts your entire bike into a waiting truck. If the bike is chained to a signpost or lightpole, he just cuts the chain (or cable) with a heavy-duty bolt cutter and the bike is free in seconds. The ultimate in security (short of having a private guard to keep thieves away) is to remove a wheel and take it with you, and chain the remains to a post with an expensive 3/8-inch high-tempered link chain, which will damage the thief's bolt cutter before it breaks. Taking off a wheel (usually the front one) is easy if you have quick-release slide-out hubs—no tools are needed. But these hubs are normally standard equipment only on the finest road and touring bikes. Unless you have a fancy bike, you will need to buy a complete new wheel to get the quick-release feature.

Generator vs. battery-powered lights. A generator has several disadvantages when compared to batteries. Since power is obtained by pressing a small wheel on the generator against the wheel rim or tire, there is a certain amount of drag created which makes pedalling slightly harder. Also, when you stop the bike, the wheels stop, the generator stops, and the lights go out. The generator is a complicated mechanism compared to batteries and therefore more subject to breakdown. And, on a first-cost basis anyway, it is more expensive. I believe the disadvantages outweigh a generator's one advantage, namely, that you don't need to replace dead batteries to keep your lights going.

Handlebar tape. Tape is generally used on turned-down handlebars to accommodate the many positions of the rider's hands. You can get plastic or cloth tape with either adhesive or non-adhesive backing. Make sure the brake levers and other accessories on your handlebars are in the position you want them before starting to tape. Start about two inches to either side of the center of the handlebars. If you are using non-adhesive tape, stick the end of it down with a small piece of adhesive tape. Then wrap the tape around the bar, working your way toward the outer end, leaving about 1/8-inch overlap between turns. Tape over and around the brake lever and other protrusions. When you get to the end of the bar, push two or three inches of tape inside the end with your fingers. Then plug the end with a bar plug which will hold the tape in place, make the job look neat, and protect you from the sharp edge of the handlebar end in the event of a fall.

Speedometers and mileage meters. These instruments tell you how fast you are riding and how many

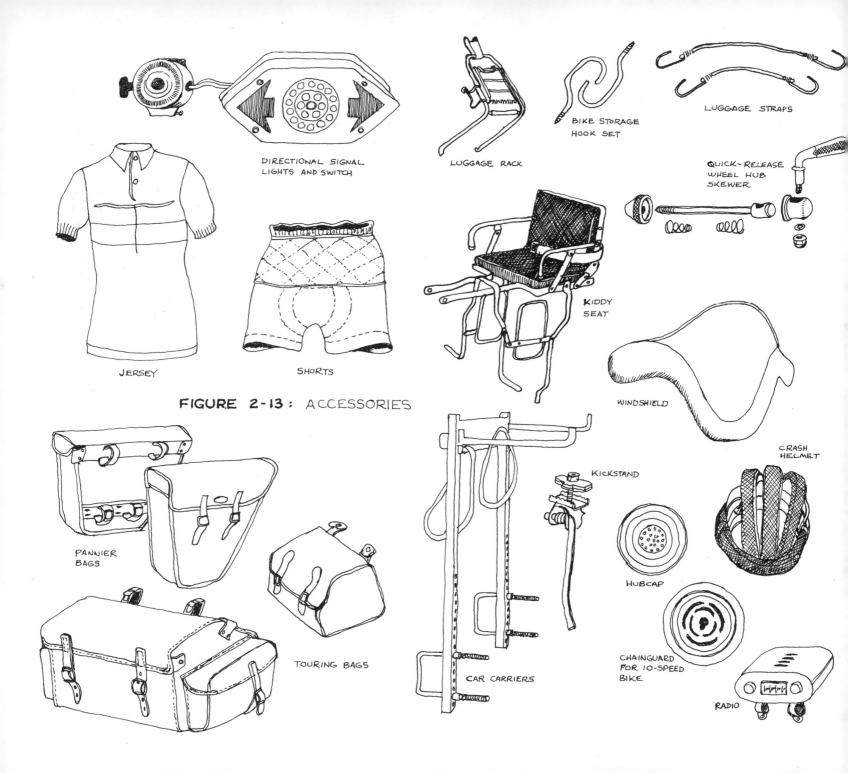

DIRECTIONAL SIGNAL LIGHTS AND SWITCH

LUGGAGE RACK

BIKE STORAGE HOOK SET

LUGGAGE STRAPS

QUICK-RELEASE WHEEL HUB SKEWER

JERSEY

SHORTS

KIDDY SEAT

WINDSHIELD

FIGURE 2-13: ACCESSORIES

CRASH HELMET

KICKSTAND

PANNIER BAGS

TOURING BAGS

CAR CARRIERS

HUBCAP

CHAINGUARD FOR 10-SPEED BIKE

RADIO

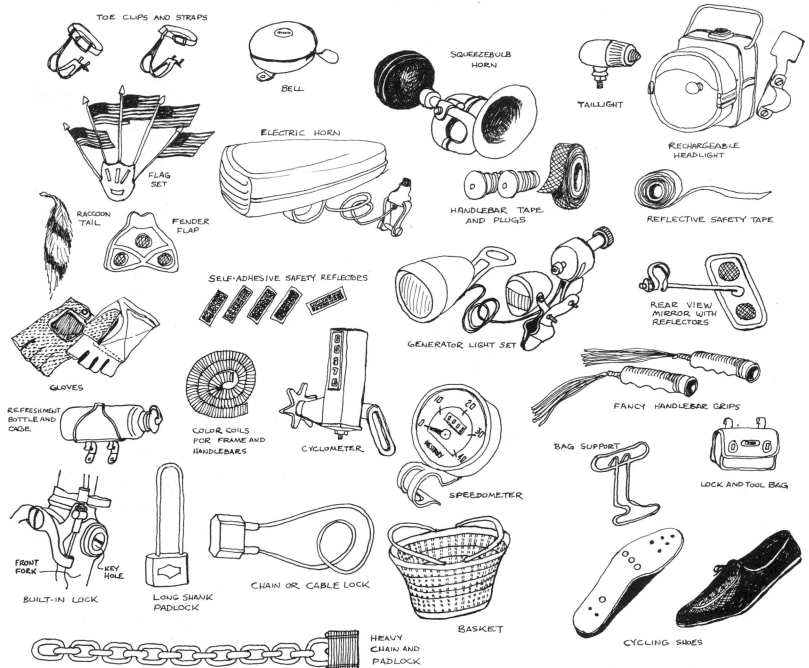

TOE CLIPS AND STRAPS

BELL

SQUEEZEBULB HORN

TAILLIGHT

RECHARGEABLE HEADLIGHT

FLAG SET

ELECTRIC HORN

HANDLEBAR TAPE AND PLUGS

REFLECTIVE SAFETY TAPE

RACCOON TAIL

FENDER FLAP

SELF-ADHESIVE SAFETY REFLECTORS

GENERATOR LIGHT SET

REAR VIEW MIRROR WITH REFLECTORS

GLOVES

REFRESHMENT BOTTLE AND CAGE

COLOR COILS FOR FRAME AND HANDLEBARS

CYCLOMETER

FANCY HANDLEBAR GRIPS

SPEEDOMETER

BAG SUPPORT

LOCK AND TOOL BAG

FRONT FORK

KEY HOLE

BUILT-IN LOCK

LONG SHANK PADLOCK

CHAIN OR CABLE LOCK

BASKET

CYCLING SHOES

HEAVY CHAIN AND PADLOCK

FIGURE 2-13: (CONTINUED)

37

miles you have covered—facts which are fun to know. Like generators, speedometers and mileage meters (also called cyclometers or odometers) take power from the bike wheel and thus cause some drag, although it is hardly noticeable. With mileage meters that use a metal striker attached to a spoke, the drag is negligible from a pedalling standpoint, but some people are annoyed by the click the striker makes with every revolution of the bike wheel. If you buy a speedometer or a mileage meter, be sure it is right for your wheel size.

If you don't have a speedometer but want to know how fast you are going, there is a way to do it. The number of complete revolutions a 27-inch wheel makes in five seconds is equal to the bike's speed in miles per hour (within 4% accuracy). So if you have a 27-inch wheel and a watch with a sweep second hand, count the wheel revolutions for a five-second period, and that's

FIGURE 2-14:
BIKE TRAILER

your speed in miles per hour. To count wheel revolutions, you can count odometer clicks, or attach a small piece of colored tape to the side of the front tire where you can see it as it goes by.

If you don't have 27-inch wheels, your actual speed will be less than your calculated speed in proportion to how much less your wheel diameter is than 27 inches. For example, if you count ten revolutions in five seconds but have 20-inch wheels, your speed isn't ten m.p.h., it's ten times 20 divided by 27, or 7.4 m.p.h.—but then, that's a lot to figure out in your head while riding!

Babyseats, Baskets, and Other Carriers. The loaded weight of any carrier on a bike except the saddle itself should not exceed about 40 pounds. Most bikes just aren't designed to carry a lot of weight in addition to the rider. If you must, place any load weighing over ten pounds over the rear wheel rather than the front wheel. Heavy loads in front will make steering harder, and possibly dangerous, by producing an "oversteer" effect. (I have a large wire basket hanging from the handlebars of my bike. When I'm pedalling home from the store with a copy of the Sunday newspaper in my basket, steering is noticeably affected. When I start to go into a turn, the weight of the paper tends to pull the handlebars further into the turn. This creates an unstable situation, requiring extra attention to steering.)

If you are planning to carry heavy loads but want to avoid the imbalance problems described above, buy a bike trailer. New lightweight, well-engineered designs are available that emphasize proper weight distribution, positive no-weave tracking, and an unrestricted turning radius. And they provide enough space to carry gear for a camping trip, a week's groceries, or a couple of small kids.

FIGURE 2-15: EXAMPLE OF AN OVERLOADED BIKE (AUTHOR, SONS, AND SUNDAY NEWSPAPER)

FIGURE 3-1: CHAINWHEEL

3

HOW TO BUY A BIKE

If you don't own a bike, or if the one you have is too small, broken down, or ancient, you may be thinking of buying a new (or used) one. If such is the case, here are a few tips that may save you money and headaches. Think about them before you take the plunge.

POINTS TO CONSIDER BEFORE PURCHASE

Why are you buying a bike? Many kids (and adults) buy bikes just for fun, exercise, and neighborhood transportation. For this kind of use, you'll probably be happy with an ordinary, not-too-fancy bike. On the other hand, if you need a bike for carrying loads such as newspapers or groceries, you'll want to consider a stronger, heavy-framed model. If you race, climb hills, tour cross-country, or ride to a distant school or office every day, you should get a lightweight bike with gears.

How long will you keep a bike? If you're still growing, chances are you will outgrow a bike in a couple of years. In this case, unless you have younger brothers or sisters who can inherit your bike, you should avoid spending too much money: if it's your first bike, it will probably be an experiment anyhow. But if you are an experienced rider, are definite about what kind of bike you want, and plan to keep it for several years or longer, spending a little more will pay in the long run.

How much storage space do you have? For those with space available in a garage, basement, or hallway, this is not a major problem. However, if you plan to keep a bike in the back of a clothes closet or carry it under the hood of a VW, you might consider a folding bike, or a lightweight bike with quick-release, slide-out wheels.

Will you give it tender loving care? A bike needs

care as much as any machine (or person) if you want to keep it functioning properly. Chapter 5 tells you how to take proper care of a bike. If you are not inclined to follow the suggestions given there, you should weigh the idea of buying a used bike that is already beat up, instead of taking a beating yourself when you go to sell or trade a poorly cared-for machine.

How much can you spend? Are you buying a bike with your own hard-earned pocket money or fru-gally saved allowance? New bikes vary widely in price: adult models begin at around $40 and can go up to more than $400 if you want top quality plus extras. A chart in the Appendix gives a representative range of base prices as of early 1972 (local taxes and accessories, if any, would be extra; base prices may vary slightly depending on area).

If money is a problem (and for most of us it is!), think seriously about getting a used bike. Doing so can

FIGURE 3-2: MEASURING RIDER AND BIKE HEIGHT

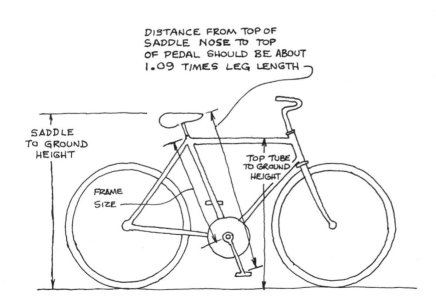

DISTANCE FROM TOP OF SADDLE NOSE TO TOP OF PEDAL SHOULD BE ABOUT 1.09 TIMES LEG LENGTH

SADDLE TO GROUND HEIGHT

FRAME SIZE

TOP TUBE TO GROUND HEIGHT

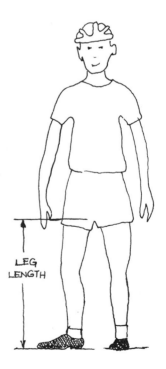

LEG LENGTH

give you some advantages, provided you study the part of this chapter on what to look for in a used bike so you don't get fleeced when you buy. One advantage is that you might be able to make money in the long run if you can find a beat-up but basically serviceable used bike, fix it up (using the fix-up hints in this book, of course), and re-sell it later. Another advantage is that even near-new used bikes usually have all the "bugs" worked out. For this reason, as well as economy, it is often better to buy a top-quality used bike in good condition than a lesser-quality new bike, even when the prices are the same.

What style do you like? That is usually a matter of personal taste, your use for the bike, and maybe even what your friends are riding. Remember that the first two considerations *should* be most important. If you are undecided on style, study what's available. Look at the pictures in this book. Look at the catalogues and floor samples at your dealer's. And don't let your friends talk you into a style you won't be happy with later on.

Where should you buy? New bikes are sold in several kinds of stores. Large department stores, sporting goods stores, discount centers, and some hardware stores and mail order outlets usually carry at least one line. The best source, however, is your nearest bicycle shop. Such places, which specialize in bikes, offer good advice on what kind of bike you should choose. They will put your new bike together for you, adjust it proper-

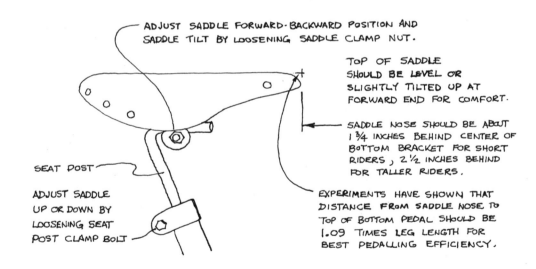

FIGURE 3-3 : ADJUSTING SADDLE POSITION

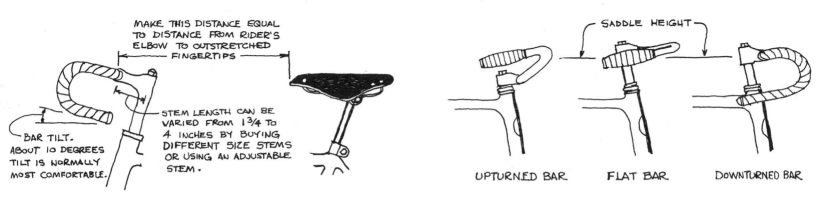

MAKE THIS DISTANCE EQUAL TO DISTANCE FROM RIDER'S ELBOW TO OUTSTRETCHED FINGERTIPS

STEM LENGTH CAN BE VARIED FROM 1¾ TO 4 INCHES BY BUYING DIFFERENT SIZE STEMS OR USING AN ADJUSTABLE STEM.

BAR TILT. ABOUT 10 DEGREES TILT IS NORMALLY MOST COMFORTABLE.

SADDLE HEIGHT

UPTURNED BAR   FLAT BAR   DOWNTURNED BAR

TILT AND STEM LENGTH RELATIVE TO SADDLE POSITION

HANDLEBAR HEIGHT RELATIVE TO SADDLE HEIGHT

FIGURE 3-4: ADJUSTING HANDLEBAR POSITION

ly, and explain the details of how to use it. (Many big discount houses and department stores won't do any of these things. They simply don't have the qualified personnel to do the job and do it right.) Bike shops will usually do repair work—efficiently and competently—after you have bought a machine from them, under any guarantee that goes with your bike. Some other kinds of shops will too, but you can't always count on it. Bike shops will usually take your old bike in trade, too, another feature other stores seldom offer. And finally, because they take trades, bike shops can show you a wide range of reconditioned used bikes as well as new ones.

Get a bike that fits! There are enough combina- tions of wheel and frame sizes so that, no matter what your size or shape, you can find a new bicycle that fits. A used one may present more of a problem because of limitations on what's available in your local area, but you should be able to find one that can be adjusted to your size.

Start out by measuring your height. If you are less than five feet tall, you need both a relatively small frame and relatively small wheels. This is especially true for the young beginner buying a boy's bike because the top tube must be comfortably close to the ground. People from five to six feet tall can use a medium to large frame with 26- or 27-inch wheels. If you're really big—six feet plus—get a large frame and 27-inch wheels. A table in the Appendix gives rule-of-thumb frame sizes based on standard 26- or 27-inch wheels.

The easiest way to fit a bike to a rider is simply to try a few bikes and see which is best by trial and error. But if for some reason you cannot try them out, or if you want to buy a bike as a gift for someone and don't want to ruin the surprise, there is a way to minimize the risk of choosing the wrong size. Measure the prospective rider's leg length from the top inside of the leg to the ground, with flat-heeled shoes on. You can then use the appropriate table in the Appendix to pick a suitable frame and wheel size with this measurement.

ADJUSTING YOUR BIKE

When you decide on the right bike, the final step before handing over the cash is to adjust (or have the shop adjust) the saddle and handlebars to match your leg and arm lengths, and take a final test ride. When the saddle position is just right, you should be able to sit on it and touch the ball of at least one foot to the ground. If only the tip of one toe touches, the seat is too high. If you can rest the flat of both your heels on the ground without strain, the seat is too low. Loosen the bolt on the frame under the saddle until you can slide the seat post up and down; then adjust the seat until you think it is right, and retighten the bolt.

Now try this for fine tuning. Rotate the pedals until one is all the way down. Sitting on the saddle, rest the ball of your foot on the bottom pedal. Can you do so comfortably? If not, adjust the seat until you can. For best pedalling efficiency, your foot should rest on the pedal as shown in Figure 3-5; your heel should be slightly higher than your toe, and your knee slightly bent.

If you adjust the seat for good pedalling efficien-

cy but can no longer touch the ground without slipping off the saddle, or if the seat is lowered as far as it will go and you're still not able to touch the ground, the bike has too large a frame for you. If the seat is as high as it will go and you can still rest your feet flat on the ground, you need a larger frame. (You may be told by your local bike dealer that it is all right for you not to be able to touch the ground while sitting in the saddle, as long as you can touch while standing up and straddling the top tube. But not all experts agree on this. Some say—and I agree—that you lose slow-riding control with the seat extremely high.)

The other two adjustments you need to make are in the handlebar position (height and angle) and the saddle forward-backward position (if your saddle permits this.) Figure 3-4 shows how these adjustments are made.

BUYING A USED BIKE

There are three basic sources for used bikes: bike shops, ads (in newspapers or on bulletin boards in schools, colleges, and stores), and friends. Bike shops usually guarantee their used bikes, and you can assume that they have at least performed routine maintenance on each one before offering it for sale. Consequently their used bike prices can be expected to be somewhat higher than the "as-is" prices offered by private individuals. Generally, a used bike from a reputable store will cost from 1/2 to 2/3 of its new retail price—with "cream puffs" in better-than-new condition running to perhaps 90% of new price.

Whether you buy from a bike shop or a private individual, you should check out the bike's condition thoroughly before you close the deal. Here's a checklist that will help you spot potential problems.

44

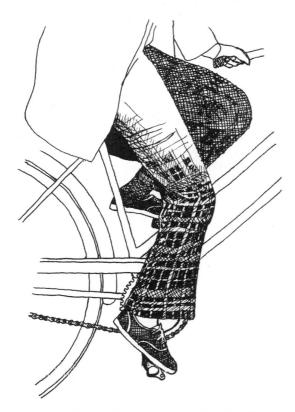

FIGURE 3-5: FOOT AND LEG POSITION FOR BEST PEDALLING EFFICIENCY.

Do the wheels spin smoothly? Turn the bike over, spin both wheels, and listen for grinding noises. Such sounds indicate that you may have to replace the bearings. If a tire wobbles from side to side when spun, the rim may need straightening.

Are the tires worn or cracked? If so, they will need replacement. Check tire (and tube) prices and add their cost to your purchase price.

Are the chain and sprockets rusty? If the rust on them is more than superficial, they may need replacement.

Do the gears shift easily? Ride the bike and try all the gears. If there are grinding noises in any gear, major repairs may be necessary.

Is the frame bent or cracked? Sight along the bike from the front and from the back. Are the frame tubes straight? A bent or crooked frame member indicates the bike may have been in an accident or had rough usage. Any cracks at joints in the frame will need repairing—and this could be expensive, depending on the extent of the damage.

Are the paint and chrome in good condition? If not, the bike has not been protected from the elements, and will begin to rust shortly, if it hasn't already started.

Will the rubber, plastic, and leather parts (handlebar grips, pedals, saddle) need replacement? If you think so, price these parts and add this to the cost.

Are all the parts and pieces there? Is the bike missing fenders, handlebar grips, or accessories you want? If it is a touring model, is it missing the built-in tire pump or the tool kit that should be strapped behind the saddle? Get an estimate of the cost to repair or replace any damaged or missing parts, and to add the accessories you want. A list of assorted bike parts appears in the Appendix with typical price ranges as of early 1972.

If you are not sure you can make a confident appraisal of the bike's condition yourself, take it to a repair shop for an expert's opinion. Some bike shops charge for this service (especially if you are not a regular customer), so ask about fees before they look it over.

BUILDING A BIKE

An alternative to buying a ready-to-roll bike is to buy the basic components described in Chapter 2 and put them together yourself. This method is tricky—one manufacturer's frame, for example, will not always fit together with the handlebars and seat made by another. You need both mechanical skills and a knowledge of bike parts to custom-build a bike.

But if you are mechanically inclined and enjoy creative tinkering, it's a lot of fun to try building your own bike. The cheapest way is to buy (or beg) a collection of used parts from a bike shop or even the local junk yard and see how well you can assemble them into a workable machine. Chapters 5 through 8 will give you some helpful guidance if you want to assemble a bike from scratch.

If you are thinking of building your own, steer away from the idea of making a "chopper-style" bike— that is, one with an extra-long, almost horizontal front fork. Handling, balancing, and steering a chopper is difficult at best, and under certain conditions can be startlingly unsafe.

For those who want a custom-built bike but are not do-it-yourselfers, there are several firms that design and build bikes to each customer's whims and specifications. This can get expensive, though. The cost runs from $200 to $500—and even higher, depending on how many made-to-order parts are required.

SPECIAL NOTES ON BUYING SMALL BEGINNERS' BIKES

Most of the subjects discussed in this book apply to all kinds of bikes, from the simplest two-wheelers to the most sophisticated ten-speed machines. But when it comes to buying a beginner's bike (12-, 16-, or 20-inch wheels on a small frame), there are some special facts you should know.

Rate of growth. This should be an important consideration, particularly for young beginners. An average five- to seven-year-old will fit a small-framed bike with 20-inch wheels. A smaller child may fit only on a 12-inch or a 16-inch model. These sizes tend to be outgrown fast. But parents should think hard before getting a bike that's too big in the belief that their child will quickly grow into it. He may be very unhappy until he does, and that may take longer than the parents think!

Frames. On beginners' bikes the frames are often constructed differently from bigger bikes. For strength, a frame should have at least two permanent frame members welded to the steering head. Frames with only one permanent member are flimsy, even when a second bolt-on member is added, for example, to make a girl's model into a boy's.

Tires. Tires should be the soft inflatable kind, not the hard non-inflatable kind. To tell one kind from the other, look for the air valve—non-inflatable tires have none. The latter also have about 15% less braking traction, are less comfortable when riding over bumpy terrain, wear much faster, and make the bike harder to pedal. In fact, rolling resistance is about three times higher with non-inflatable than with inflatable tires.

46

Ball bearings. These are important and are not built into every bike. Some inexpensive models have plain bearings (such as plastic sleeves) in the pedals and steering head. These bearings make pedalling harder and impair handling ease and stability. Steering, particularly, is harder without ball bearings in the front end. The reason is that plain bearings cause enough binding to slow the normally instant front wheel response to the rider's movements. You can perform an easy experiment to test steering "freeness." Hold the test bike by the front of its frame and lift the front wheel clear of the ground. Start the wheel spinning and tilt the bike left or right. If the steering is all right, the handlebars should turn freely in the direction the bike is tilted. Another test: "no-hands" riding is often difficult or impossible without ball bearings in the steering head.

Pedals. On beginners' bikes (and all others) the pedals should be rubber, not plastic. Plastic can be unusually slippery, even against sneakers.

Coaster brakes and gearshift. Young beginners who don't have the coordination, strength, or finger span to operate handbrake and gear levers should use coaster brakes and put off having a gearshift until they are older. Usually kids reach the age of 12 or 14 before they can really master the derailleur operation. Shifting three-speed gears is slightly easier, and a well-coordinated child of ten can handle it. For bicyclists with good coordination but a small finger span, dual position caliper brakes are a help. These have a pair of auxiliary levers placed close to the handlebars for easier squeezing.

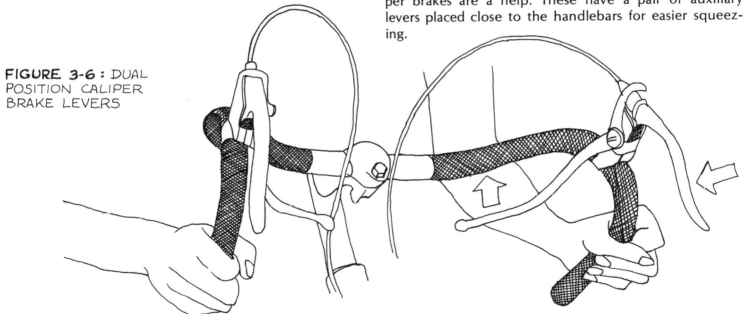

FIGURE 3-6 : DUAL POSITION CALIPER BRAKE LEVERS

Training wheels. Training wheels are a short-term learning aid for the four- to seven-year-old group. They are strictly optional; many kids have learned to ride without them. But they do give the rider a feel for pedalling, braking, and steering without having to worry about balancing. Another advantage of training wheels is that a child who hasn't grown into his two-wheeler yet can still use it, with the training wheels, without loss of control.

Adjustments. Check the range of up-and-down saddle adjustment. It largely determines how soon a growing rider will outgrow the bike. Figure that at least

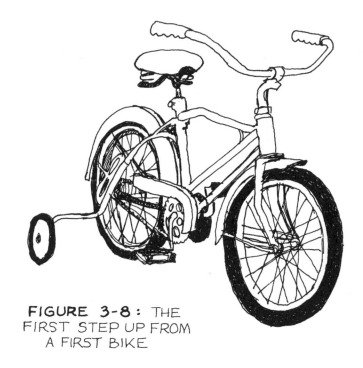

FIGURE 3-8: THE FIRST STEP UP FROM A FIRST BIKE

FIGURE 3-7: A GOOD FIRST BIKE

two inches of seat post should stay inside the seat tube for safe, sure support. Another four inches or more of vertical adjustment is a minimum, so the seat post should be at least six inches long.

Remember, too, that as the seat is adjusted upward, the handlebars will need to be moved up too. Most handlebars have a lot less height adjustment than saddles—often only an inch or two. But check to see that there is at least this much to work with. One other difference among handlebar designs is that most can be angled upward or downward, but some are welded in at a fixed angle and this also limits adjustment flexibility.

4

HOW TO RIDE A BIKE
(For Beginners and Experts)

Most of you probably know how to ride a bike, but there's no harm in checking your technique. And if you haven't learned to ride yet, you will be able to do it right the first time, using the guidance given in this chapter.

FOR THE NOVICE

How old should you be to learn? I have heard of mere lads of four suddenly shucking their training wheels and scooting off unassisted on two-wheelers. But this is rare. Most children can learn to ride a two-wheeler around the age of five or six, if they are given the opportunity. And, of course, some people learn much later in life.

Balancing. If you have never ridden before, but are a reasonably well-coordinated person at least six or seven years old, you can probably learn quite easily. If possible, it is best to learn to ride on a conventional bicycle rather than something fancy, such as a high-riser. The somewhat awkward position of the handlebars and the smaller wheels make steering harder, even for the experienced rider.

There are various ways to learn bike riding. However, only one method will be discussed here—one which is effective, simple, and quick. First, you need a hill that has a *very gentle* slope. A long driveway is ideal. If you choose a road, it should be reasonably free of traffic, gravel, and potholes.

When you have found a suitable hill, push your bike 20 or 30 feet up from the bottom. Aim it downhill and sit astride the saddle, holding yourself steady with the balls of your feet on the ground. Now comes the moment of truth. Keeping both feet close to the ground for balance, gently push yourself forward. You're rolling! Steer straight ahead. You can drag your feet along the road if it helps your balance. Look straight ahead, not down at your feet. Don't worry about the pedals yet; they will take care of themselves. If the hill is gentle and short enough, you don't have to worry about using the brakes; you can always stop with your feet.

You get to the bottom with no problems. Go back up the hill and try it again. And keep trying until you can coast all the way down without dragging your feet at all. When you can do that, you have learned how to balance.

Steering. Now ride down the hill again, only this time pay more attention to your steering. If it is your first time out, you are probably shaky, and the following hints may be helpful.

Try pedalling. Many people find steering is easier if they're pumping the pedals. In general, the faster you go (up to a normal cruising speed of 15 miles per hour), the easier it is to steer. So after you learn to pedal, don't crawl along. Go!

And don't be nervous. You'll be surprised how much easier it is to steer when your arm muscles are relaxed, not all tensed up.

Getting on. There are several acceptable ways of getting onto the saddle of a bike. The easiest is to straddle your bike first. Then stroke the forward pedal with one foot, simultaneously pushing off with the other foot and raising yourself onto the saddle, using your grip on the handlebars to steady yourself. This is the method recommended for beginners.

After you gain some experience, you may want to use the "flying start." For this method, stand on the left side of the bike with your hands on the grips, put your left foot on the left pedal, and push the bike forward with your right foot. (The tricky part is to balance the bike while you are in this position.) Then, as you are rolling along, swing your right foot casually backward up and over the saddle as if you were mounting a horse, sit down, and you are on (and off).

IMPROVING YOUR TECHNIQUE

Once you have learned how to pedal around the block a couple of times untouched by other human hands, you are ready to learn some of the bicycling techniques the experts use. Learned properly, these techniques will help keep you from getting that tired, worn-out feeling on long bike trips. Here are several to keep in mind.

Ankling. This term refers to the way you should flex your ankles as you ride to maintain a steady pressure on the pedals. For proper ankling, place only the ball of your foot, not your arch, on the pedal. When the pedal is at the top of its swing, your toe should be pointing slightly upward, and the ball of your foot should be pushing the pedal forward and down. When the pedal is at the bottom of its swing, your toe should be pointing downward at about a 45-degree angle, the ball of your foot pushing the pedal back and up. Even without toe clips and straps, you should be able to apply pedal pressure backwards for some distance after the pedal starts to rise (until it is about at the 7:00 o'clock position for your right foot, 5:00 o'clock for your left).

Ankling should be a smooth, continuous movement from top to bottom, never jerky. Pressure should be applied steadily from top to bottom, tapering in and out at both ends of the power stroke.

Cadence. This is the beat or pace of pedalling—the relatively constant crank rotation speed with which the rider is most comfortable and effective. A pace that can be maintained comfortably by most teenagers and adults over a long time period is 65 to 85 strokes (or crank revolutions) per minute. If you have gears, it is particularly important to use them to help maintain your natural cadence. You will find that pedalling for

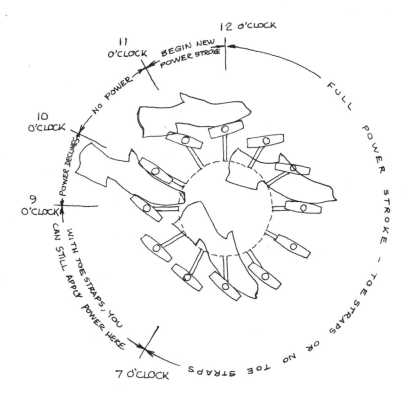

11 O'CLOCK

12 O'CLOCK

BEGIN NEW POWER STROKE

NO POWER

10 O'CLOCK

FULL POWER STROKE — TOE STRAPS OR NO TOE STRAPS

POWER DECLINES

9 O'CLOCK

WITH TOE STRAPS, YOU CAN STILL APPLY POWER HERE

7 O'CLOCK

FIGURE 4-1: ANKLING TECHNIQUE

any length of time at a pace which is either faster or slower than that which comes naturally will tire you out.

Posting. "Posting" is standing on the pedals, up off the saddle with your knees bent, ready to absorb approaching bumps. The knack of posting comes almost instinctively after you have been slapped by your saddle a couple of times riding over rough terrain. It improves rider comfort and, incidentally, is easier on the bike.

Hard pumping. It hardly needs mentioning that when you climb a steep hill without benefit of a low gear, you will find it hard to pump the pedals. What is the most effective pedalling style under these conditions? Here is one that will give you a short burst of pedalling power. Stand straight up on the pedals so that your *full weight* is applied to pushing each pedal down in turn. Then, with your back and arms straight, try to pull the handlebars upward. You will find you can apply terrific pressure on the pedals using this technique, enough, in fact, to bend the pedal spindles or pull the rear wheel out of line if you're not careful! You will also find that it's a very tiring way to travel. If you do a lot of hill climbing, you will have to choose between getting tired, walking your bike up the hill, or getting a suitably geared machine.

Changing gears. If you don't have a gearshift on your bike, naturally you don't need to worry about changing gears. But if you do have gears, remember that you should pedal gently when shifting. Don't pump, coast, or back-pedal. Not observing this rule will tend to make shifting harder and can damage the gear mechanism.

Although you *must* be moving and pedalling to shift derailleur gears, with the epicyclic rear hub you can change gears with your bike stopped. To do this, rest the weight of your foot (not too much—just enough to make shifting easy) on the upper forward pedal while you shift. And don't force the shifting lever—move it gently. If you have a derailleur-equipped bike but don't know how to shift, study Figure 2-9 on pages 30-31 which shows how this mechanism works.

SAFE BICYCLING: RULES OF THE ROAD

The Basic Rule of the Road is simple: *Stay out of the other guy's way.* Most other rules are extensions of and ways to accomplish this. Here are some of them.

Keep to the right. Follow traffic. Keeping to the right—that is, riding with the traffic rather than against it—*is the law in every state in the U.S.A.*

Don't swerve or weave. Unexpected moves can cause accidents. Stay as close to the edge of the road as you can.

Ride single file. On the average road, a car can pass a single line of riders without going into the oncoming lane. Two or more bicyclists riding abreast force cars to wait for oncoming traffic before passing.

Keep away from cars. Watch out for suddenly opening doors of parked cars, and for drivers pulling out of side streets unexpectedly.

Be careful at intersections. Look right and left before crossing. Go slow.

Obey traffic regulations. Observe and follow the directions of all stop signs, red and green lights, and other highway signs, just as if your bike were a motor vehicle. Although many people don't realize it, this is a *law* that applies to bicycles as well as motor vehicles in most states.

Watch out for pedestrians. Yield the right of way to people on foot. Remember, they can't move as fast as you can.

Use hand signals. When turning or stopping in traffic, let other drivers know your intent.

Never "hitch" rides. This means never hanging onto a moving automobile or truck and letting it tow your bike. Don't do it: it's dangerous.

Don't overload your bike. Don't carry too much extra weight, and never ride double. Unless it is a tandem, your bike was not designed to carry more than one person.

Don't try to do "tricks" with your bike. For example, "popping a wheelie" (riding with the bike's front wheel off the ground) can be dangerous if you fall backwards onto hard pavement. To avoid the risk, don't try it.

Keep your bike "safety-ready." Have proper front and rear lights and a horn or bell for signalling. Check your brakes—be sure they work efficiently and safely. Keep your tire pressure at its proper level and your bike mechanically fit. You will enjoy biking more, and the bike itself will last longer.

Check your local town rules. Many towns and cities require bicycle licenses, and have regulations prohibiting, for example, riding on sidewalks or parking bikes in certain places. Ask your police department about these.

Why you keep to the right. The first rule mentioned above is: *Keep to the right.* Of all the Rules of the Road, it's one of the most important, but unfortunately the least well known and most often disregarded. The reason for the rule is easy to understand. Think of a car driving along a winding road at 30 miles per hour. The driver is anticipating meeting cars coming around bends so he is keeping close to the right side of the road. Suddenly he sees you coming toward him on your bike. You are disregarding the law by keeping to your left instead of your right and thus are approaching him head-on in the same lane. If you are going toward him at 15 miles per hour, you are approaching each other at a relative speed of 45 miles per hour. If he first sees you when you are 88 feet away, he has 1.3 seconds to swerve out of your way. That's not much time.

On the other hand, if you are traveling in the same direction as the car and keeping to the right as you should, your speed relative to the car will be 15 miles per hour. The driver will have four seconds to move out and pass you, three times as long a period for his reflexes to react. It's as simple as that.

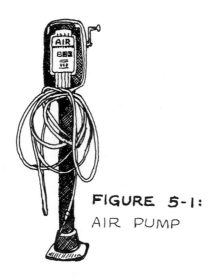

FIGURE 5-1:
AIR PUMP

5

BASIC CARE OF YOUR BIKE

You may not have the time, patience, or inclination to fix your bike when something goes wrong with it, or even to keep it fully lubricated (which is more complicated than you might think). If fixing broken gearshift cables and repacking greasy wheel bearings is not your bag, don't feel badly. There are lots of others like you. Just make sure you take your bike to a serviceman once or twice a year for mechanical inspection, lubrication, and any adjustments that might be needed. Glance at the next two chapters anyway (on lubrication and repairs you can make) in case you get stuck in the middle of a desert with no serviceman around and have no choice except to fix your bike yourself. But, even if you are not handy with tools and want to stay that way, there are still certain things you, and only you, should

do to keep your bike in good shape. This chapter covers these do-it-yourself "musts."

MAINTENANCE

Cleaning and polishing. Cleaning and polishing your bike is simple. Use a soft damp cloth (like a washcloth, diaper, or old undershirt—but check with the lady of the house first!) to wipe mud, dust, and grease off the painted and chromed parts of your bike every month or so, or more often if you can't seem to keep it from getting messy. In addition, wax all these parts three or four times a year—including once just before you store your bike for the winter (if you do). There is one exception: if your bike has caliper brakes, don't use wax on the sides of the wheel rims; doing so will affect brake operation. Liquid wax, rather than paste wax, is recommended because it is easier to spread on. Follow the waxing directions on the wax container. They usually say: apply with a soft cloth, let dry to a haze, and rub off with another soft cloth. So keep a supply of soft cloths on hand.

Riding and storing. To avoid undue mechanical trouble and rapid deterioration, be kind and gentle to your bike. Treat it like a friend. For example, avoid riding over the edges of curbs. This could damage your tires, rims, frame, and bearings. Instead, dismount and walk the bike over curbs.

Tire damage and excessive wear can also result from riding double, making skidding stops, and riding on rough pavement or over debris.

If you have gears, make sure you know what you are doing *before* you try shifting, even once.

Try to keep your bike as dry as possible. Don't ride through water or in the rain if you can help it. If you do get your bike wet, wipe it off with a dry cloth or paper towels as soon as you can. If your chain gets wet, follow the directions given later in this chapter.

Don't let your bike fall over when parking it—especially on the chain side. Use your kickstand or a bicycle rack, or lean it against something solid.

Store your bike in a dry place, preferably out of the way of things that could bump into it and cause damage. Hanging your bike on hooks from the garage ceiling is a handy way of dealing with the storage problem—particularly when you're laying it away for the winter.

Don't let your bike stand for any length of time on deflated tires—the weight may crack the sidewalls.

Tires and tubes. Keep tires and tubes inflated to their proper pressure, which is usually indicated on the sidewalls. If the sidewalls don't give this figure, the Tire Pressure Table in the Appendix may be helpful. (Note: If you happen to be putting air in the tires of a tandem bike, increase the pressures shown in the table by 10 to 20 pounds to handle the extra weight of bike and riders.)

The pressures shown are recommended for average loads. If the load is heavier than average, or if your tires bulge more than slightly when the bike is moving, add about five pounds more pressure.

Check occasionally to make sure your valve cores are tight and don't leak. Keep the valve stems straight; they become crooked from riding on underinflated tires.

When tires and tubes get to be six to eight years old, the rubber begins to harden and crack. If yours are getting this ancient, it's time to replace them.

Be careful if you use a gas station pressure tank to pump up your tires. Bike tires are so small that they hold very little air, and are therefore very easy to overinflate and even explode by leaving the air hose on too long. Set the pump pressure regulator *below* your minimum need. Attach the hose just momentarily—a couple of seconds at most—and then remove it. Check the pressure with a hand tire pressure gauge. The station attendant will usually have one if you don't. If it reads less than the pressure you want, give it another squirt, gradually inching up the regulator to the pressure your tire needs. Remember, if the pump regulator is not accurate (and a lot of them aren't) and you leave the hose on too long, you may have a blowout. One way to avoid "gas-station-tire-pump nerves" is to use a hand-operated pump. Even with this, however, you can overinflate and blow out a tire, but you will have to work hard to do it.

Brakes. Test your brakes regularly. Adjust or repair them (or have it done) promptly if they go out of whack, for obvious safety reasons.

Chain. Check the chain adjustment. If it is too tight, it will bind and make pedalling harder; if it is too loose, it may strain the links and even come off. Adjust the chain so it has about ⅜-inch play. Figure 5-2 shows how. (Note: If your chain is loose, it's usually because the rear wheel has slipped forward in the frame slots rather than because the chain itself has stretched. Loosen the rear hub nuts and pull back on the wheel until the chain is correctly adjusted. Then re-tighten the nuts.)

Other components. Make sure wheel nuts, saddle, and handlebars are securely tightened, for your own safety. Check all bike components and replace them, or have them replaced, if they are broken or badly worn. For example, check the pedals (worn pedals can be dangerously slippery); check the spokes (loose or broken spokes cause rim distortion); and check the handlebar grips (loose, broken, or missing grips can be a safety hazard). Inspect accessories such as lights, horns, and bells to be sure they work. If your batteries seem low, replace them before they give out completely. Replace broken or missing reflectors, too. Finally, if you are growing, re-adjust the handlebar and saddle heights periodically.

EASY-TO-DO LUBRICATION

There are a few parts of the lubricating job that you can do without using tools or acquiring any special knowledge or skills. All you need is an oil can (preferably of the thumb-pumping variety) filled with light oil. You can buy this oil at your local gas station, or get bike oil ready-packed in a can with a spout from your bike shop. Don't use vegetable-base oil because it can dry up and leave a gunky residue.

Coaster brakes and internally geared hubs. You will probably find an oil hole on your rear wheel hub if

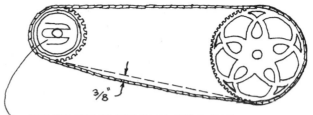

ADJUST CHAIN TENSION BY SLIDING REAR AXLE FORWARD OR BACKWARD IN REAR DROPOUT SLOT.

FIGURE 5-2: PROPER CHAIN ADJUSTMENT

you have a coaster brake or three-speed bike. Squirt a few drops of oil into the hole once a month. If you have an internally geared hub with an indicator chain sticking out the side, place a drop or two on this chain. Also put a drop on the hand control at the other end of the control cable, and a drop where the cable enters the "spaghetti tubing."

Caliper brakes. If you have caliper brakes, lightly oil the pivot bolt between the brake arms every 30 days. (But don't get oil on the wheel rims or brake pads!)

Derailleur mechanisms. If you have a derailleur-equipped bike, occasionally wipe off the derailleur with a clean rag; don't let dirt and grime accumulate there. Put one drop of oil on the pivot bolts every 30 days. More oil than that is unnecessary and would just attract dirt.

Chain. Because the chain is usually covered with sticky oil, is close to the ground where dust is apt to linger, and is positioned so that the front wheel throws dirt into it, it can get quite gunky. You'll have to work on it frequently to keep it well oiled and clean. You can use either a light machine oil or a silicone dry lubricant. Silicone lubricant comes in a spray can and dries like wax, and dirt won't stick to it. (But if you decide to use silicone, you must remove *all* the oil from the chain and sprockets first.) Turn the bike upside down and slowly rotate the crank lubricating each section of the chain as it becomes exposed. If you use oil, wipe the excess off with a rag; an over-oiled chain will collect extra dust and dirt and get gunkier faster. If you are starting out with an especially dirty chain, a preliminary wipe with some kerosene on a rag will help. Or you might want to take the chain off and soak it in kerosene: Chapter 7 explains how to do this. If you get your chain wet and have chosen to use regular oil rather than silicone, use penetrating oil to force the water out from between the links, then oil it in the regular way. You don't need to worry about a wet chain if you have it well lubricated with silicone lubricant, since the silicone repels water.

Weird noises. If a strange klunk, squeal, or click suddenly develops that wasn't there before, don't keep riding your bike hoping it will go away. Figure out what's causing the problem and fix it, or take it to your bike shop and let them figure it out and fix it. If you don't, you may turn the need for a minor adjustment or lubrication into a major and expensive overhaul.

There it is: that's all there is to the basic care of your bike. Follow these simple guidelines and you'll keep your bike in good shape and your friendly serviceman occasionally entertained. If you don't care about entertaining your serviceman, you can try doing some of the easier maintenance and repair work yourself, giving only the really tough jobs to the bike shop. The next three chapters describe the tools you will need and what you can do with them.

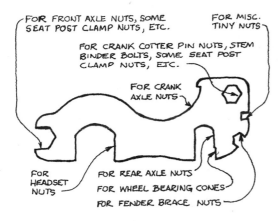

FOR FRONT AXLE NUTS, SOME SEAT POST CLAMP NUTS, ETC.

FOR MISC. TINY NUTS

FOR CRANK COTTER PIN NUTS, STEM BINDER BOLTS, SOME SEAT POST CLAMP NUTS, ETC.

FOR CRANK AXLE NUTS

FOR HEADSET NUTS

FOR REAR AXLE NUTS

FOR WHEEL BEARING CONES

FOR FENDER BRACE NUTS

FIGURE 6-1: ALL-PURPOSE SPANNER

6

TOOLS:
For Service and Repair

Luckily, most of the tools you will need to disassemble or adjust your bike are small. You won't need big, heavy screwdrivers suitable for prying open safes or tremendous, weapon-like wrenches. Thus you can store bike tools in a small drawer or box, or even carry them with you. If you have a touring bike, you may find it already equipped with a handy leather (or plastic) tool kit strapped behind the saddle. This kit is usually filled with a variety of goodies, but it won't necessarily have everything you want. If you have such a tool kit, check it against the items below.

TOOLS FOR DISMANTLING AND ADJUSTING

A decent set of wrenches. You can buy wrenches (called "spanners" in England) that are designed to fit the nuts on your bike. Caution: if you have a foreign-built bike, or an American bike with some foreign parts, at least some of its nuts and bolts are probably metric sizes. American wrenches, designed for fasteners sized in inches, won't fit them properly. If you try to force an American wrench on a European nut you will probably strip the corners or "flats" off the nut. For less than a dollar in any good bike store, you can buy a couple of "bicycle spanners" that will fit most nuts and bolts on your bike. Get an all-purpose spanner plus a dumbbell wrench (shown in Figure 6-2).

You may want a thin offset wrench especially designed for adjusting the hub bearing cones in your

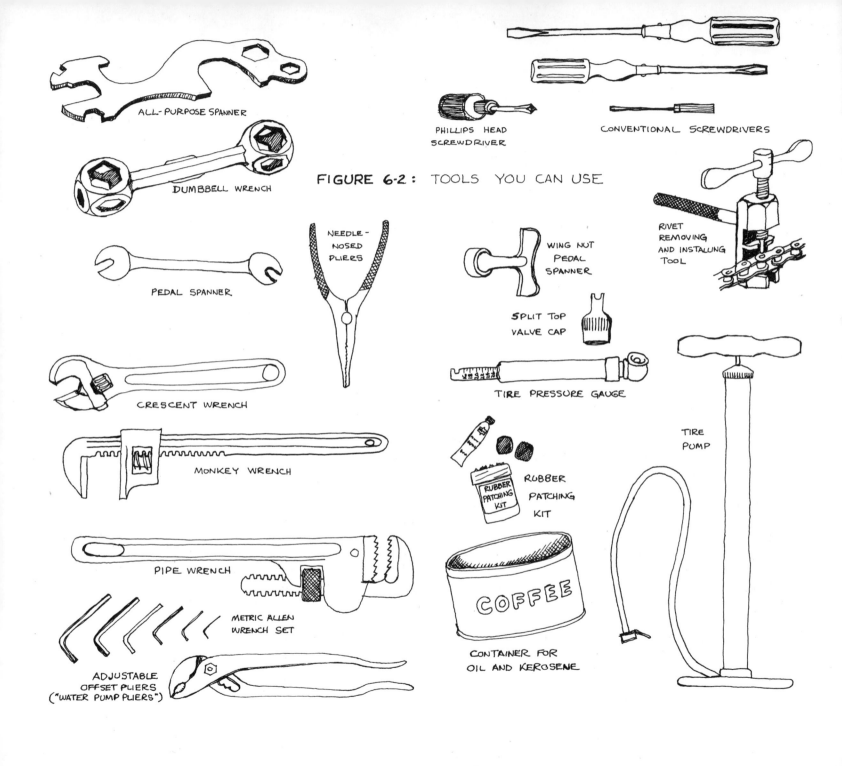

FIGURE 6·2: TOOLS YOU CAN USE

ALL-PURPOSE SPANNER

DUMBBELL WRENCH

PEDAL SPANNER

NEEDLE-NOSED PLIERS

CRESCENT WRENCH

MONKEY WRENCH

PIPE WRENCH

METRIC ALLEN WRENCH SET

ADJUSTABLE OFFSET PLIERS ("WATER PUMP PLIERS")

PHILLIPS HEAD SCREWDRIVER

CONVENTIONAL SCREWDRIVERS

WING NUT PEDAL SPANNER

SPLIT TOP VALVE CAP

TIRE PRESSURE GAUGE

RUBBER PATCHING KIT

RUBBER PATCHING KIT

CONTAINER FOR OIL AND KEROSENE

COFFEE

RIVET REMOVING AND INSTALING TOOL

TIRE PUMP

wheels. (This wrench is optional, but costs only a couple of dollars and is nice to have if you are constantly fussing with bearing adjustments.)

A crescent wrench is handy to have in your tool bin, but even the smaller sizes are too bulky to be a good substitute for bicycle spanners. If you do use one, be careful. If not properly adjusted, it can strip the corners off hex (six-sided) nuts and bolts, making removal very difficult.

A pedal wrench is designed especially to fit the flats on the pedal spindle. It isn't indispensible, but it may save you some pedal-removing time.

A spoke wrench is handy to have for fixing or adjusting your spokes.

If you have derailleur gears and want to work on them, you will probably also need a metric Allen wrench set but, as you will see in the next chapter, I don't recommend taking the derailleur mechanism apart unless you are really mechanically inclined.

Pliers. A small pair of needle-nosed pliers and a pair of heavy-duty offset pliers are handy to have in your tool bin, though they're not absolutely necessary.

Three or four screwdrivers. You're likely to find uses for at least three screwdrivers: one tiny, one medium-sized, and one large. In addition, you may need one or two Phillips head screwdrivers. Check the screw heads on your bike to make sure.

A rivet extracting and installing tool. This costs about $4.00 and is needed for a derailleur-equipped bike with a 3/32-inch wide chain. (Non-derailleur bikes generally have 1/8-inch wide chains that can be taken apart by prying off a snap link with thin-nosed pliers or a screwdriver blade.

TOOLS FOR TIRE AND WHEEL WORK

Split-top valve caps. These are used to remove or tighten tire valve cores. A valve cap is not strictly a tool, but you use it like one when you are fixing your valves. Before you go out and buy a set, look at your bike. Your tires may already be equipped with split-top caps.

A tire pressure gauge. This looks like a fat pencil and has a hole in one end that the tire valve is pressed into. Air pressure from the tire is released through this hole and pushes a metal stick out the opposite end of the gauge. The stick has numbers on it which indicate air pressure. A pressure gauge costs from $1.50 to $4.00 depending on the range of pressure readings. Normally, gas stations have these on hand for checking automobile tire pressure, so you can probably borrow one from an attendant if you don't have one.

A hand-operated tire pump. As explained in the last chapter, using a hand pump to fill your tires can prevent overinflating and even exploding them. A hand pump is relatively inexpensive, and gives you the convenience of inflating your tires at home instead of lugging your bike to a gas station.

A rubber patching kit. Patching your own leaks in your tires can be less expensive and quicker than asking a serviceman to do it.

LAST BUT NOT LEAST

An open container of kerosene. A wide-mouthed coffee can or deep pie plate makes a good "bathtub" for soaking dirty bike chains and other parts in kerosene.

An open container of light oil. This can be used for soaking your bike chain if you use oil as a chain lubricant. If you use silicone lubricant instead (and I recommend you do), you don't need a container of this type.

A couple of rags. These are necessary for wiping oil away and for cleaning up after major, or minor, surgery. For this purpose, a baby's diaper is ideal. If you can filch one without the baby noticing, roll it up tight and stow it in your tool pouch for future use.

A large clean cloth to lay parts on. When you begin taking pieces of your bike apart, you should lay out each piece in a line on a large, clean cloth just as you remove it. Then, when it is time to reassemble, you will be sure that all the pieces are going back just as they came off. *Don't* throw all the pieces into a shoe box, hoping you'll remember how they go back together. You might not.

Tools you don't need. There are a great variety of bicycle tools not listed above which are used for special purposes or to make life easier for the professional bike repairman. Crank straighteners, cup-fastening tools, wheel assembly tools, and wheel lifters are a few of the odd tools that fit into this category. A representative selection is shown in Figure 6-3. You won't need any of them for the work described in this book, but you might be interested to know that such items exist.

Work space. A workshop or work area in your basement or garage, preferably with a tool bench having a bolted-down vise, is the best place to operate. Hopefully, this will be an out-of-the-way place where you can leave greasy parts without fear of their getting kicked around, dusty, or rained on. This is important, since the jobs that are described in the next chapter often take longer than you think, especially for a beginner.

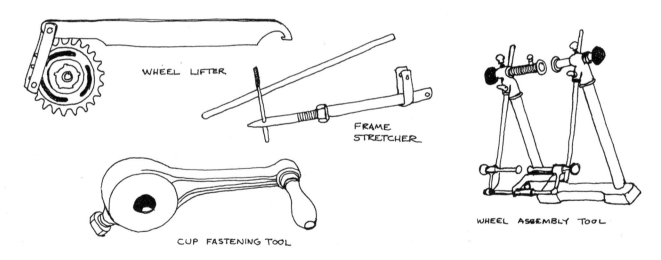

WHEEL LIFTER

FRAME STRETCHER

CUP FASTENING TOOL

WHEEL ASSEMBLY TOOL

FIGURE 6-3: A SAMPLING OF PROFESSIONAL BIKE REPAIR TOOLS

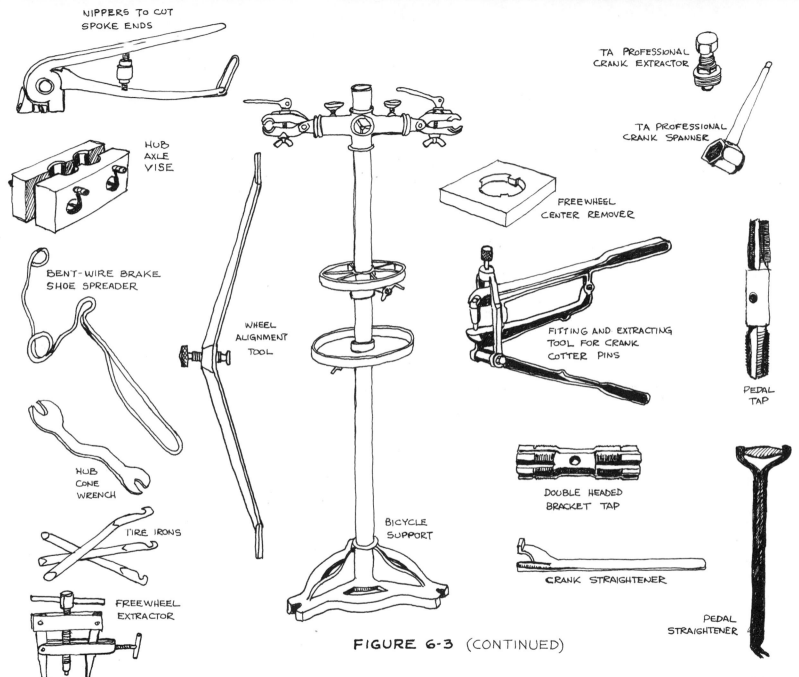

NIPPERS TO CUT SPOKE ENDS

TA PROFESSIONAL CRANK EXTRACTOR

TA PROFESSIONAL CRANK SPANNER

HUB AXLE VISE

FREEWHEEL CENTER REMOVER

BENT-WIRE BRAKE SHOE SPREADER

WHEEL ALIGNMENT TOOL

FITTING AND EXTRACTING TOOL FOR CRANK COTTER PINS

PEDAL TAP

HUB CONE WRENCH

TIRE IRONS

BICYCLE SUPPORT

DOUBLE HEADED BRACKET TAP

CRANK STRAIGHTENER

FREEWHEEL EXTRACTOR

PEDAL STRAIGHTENER

FIGURE 6-3 (CONTINUED)

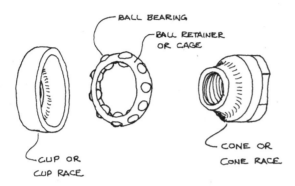

7

Labels: BALL BEARING, BALL RETAINER OR CAGE, CUP OR CUP RACE, CONE OR CONE RACE

FIGURE 7-1: PARTS OF A BEARING

HOW TO LUBRICATE YOUR BIKE

As mentioned before, if you don't have the inclination to do a complete lube job on your bike, you can squirt a little oil here and there and let your friendly serviceman do the rest. But if you yearn to see the gooey insides of your bike and don't mind buying the tools and supplies so you can do the job right, the following instructions may keep you from making too many false moves.

Plan your lubricating schedule so that one complete lube job takes place in the early spring, or at whatever time your bike's peak period of usage begins. As you will see, some parts need lubrication every couple of weeks if you ride a lot, while others can go without attention for up to six months or even longer if you don't ride much and keep away from dust, dirt and water.

Let's start with the front wheel hub, which is fairly quick and easy to take apart and lubricate. It will give you a feel for the kind of work required to lubricate your bike fully. If you can do the front wheel, you can probably do the rest of the bike, too. However, if you have trouble getting the front hub apart and back together again properly, even after studying the text and pictures in this chapter, you need more guidance. Take the bike to a serviceman or ask a more experienced mechanic-type friend to help you.

FRONT WHEEL HUB

If the hub has an oil fitting, squirt in about a half-teaspoonful of light oil every 30 to 60 days. If there is a grease fitting instead of an oil fitting, use a grease gun or a pre-packed tube of good, low-temperature multi-purpose grease. You can tell a grease fitting from an oil fitting by the size of the lubricant hole—the grease fitting hole is too small to easily squirt oil into. Give the grease fitting a couple of shots every 30 to 60 days.

Once or twice a year the hub should be taken apart, all the old grease or oil cleaned off, and relubricated with new grease. (If there is no grease or oil fitting, this is the only way the bearings will ever get lubricated.) Here is a step-by-step rundown on how to do the job. Look at Figure 7-2 as you read.

(1) Turn your bike upside down by lifting the entire thing off the ground, turning it over in mid-air and setting it down so it is resting on its handlebars and saddle. Be careful not to scrape sprockets, chain, or other delicate parts against the ground while you are doing this.

(2) Unscrew both axle nuts and their accompanying washers, and put them aside on the clean cloth you have spread out for this purpose.

(3) If you have a basket or other gimmick supported by struts running to the front axle, you will have to spread the struts and shove them out of the way.

(4) Note the position of the wheel. It should be centered in the front fork, with the tire an equal distance from each side of the fork. Spin the wheel with your hand. It shouldn't wobble, but should continue to rotate smoothly for quite a few seconds after you let go. (To give you an idea of how long "quite a few seconds" is, I have measured the spinning time for my front wheel. From the time my hand leaves the tire, having given it an energetic shove, until the wheel comes to a complete rest takes about 50 seconds.) Work the wheel back and forth on the bearings. Feel how easy (or how hard) it is to turn. It should be easy. If it is hard, the

bearings are out of adjustment, dirty, or in need of replacement.

(5) Lift the wheel out of the slots in the fork. If you have caliper brakes, you will need to hold the brake shoes apart so the wheel rim and tire can be slipped out and back in. You can get a bent-wire brake shoe spreader to do this job for you (see Figure 6-3), or you can simply use your fingers. And some fancy bikes come with a "quick-release brake lever" that, when actuated, automatically spreads apart the brake shoes.

(6) Unscrew the bearing cones and remove the ball bearings. Put all the parts on your clean cloth in order of their removal.

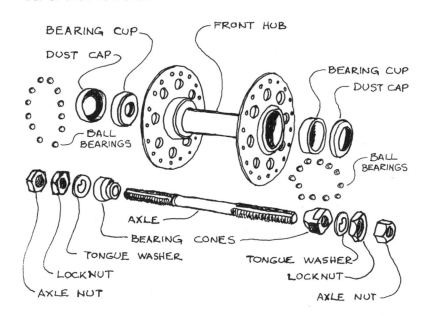

FIGURE 7-2: EXPLODED VIEW, FRONT WHEEL HUB

(7) Clean the parts one at a time in a container of kerosene. You won't be able to dip the wheel hub itself into the kerosene, so twist a kerosene-soaked rag into a rope and pull it through the axle hole a couple of times. Make sure that, when you finish, the cups (the parts of the hub the bearings ride on) are spotlessly clean.

(8) Examine the bearings, cones, and hub for wear. Buy new parts if the old ones are worn—they are surprisingly inexpensive. If all the parts still look good, make sure you have gotten them clean, then smear them with fresh grease. (Don't be afraid to get your hands greasy. Afterwards you can wipe most of the grease off with dry paper towels, and get rid of the residue with soap and water and a nail file.)

(9) Reinstall all the parts you took off, in reverse order. Be careful to adjust the bearing cones properly. If they are too tight, the wheel will slow down quickly when you give it the spin test. If they are too loose, the wheel will wobble on the axle. In either case, bearing wear will be greatly accelerated, and you don't want to keep taking the wheel apart to replace the bearings, even if they *are* cheap. So be careful.

(10) A note of caution: When dismantling your bike to clean and grease the bearings, check carefully whether the ball bearings are loose or in cages. If they are loose, *count them* before removing. And don't lose any! This applies to all maintenance requiring the removal of any bearings: on wheels, crank assemblies, or front forks. Usually the wheel bearings are in cages, but often the crank bearings and front fork bearings are loose.

REAR WHEEL HUB

Epicyclic-geared hubs (such as Sturmey-Archer or Shimano) or coaster brake hubs should not be taken

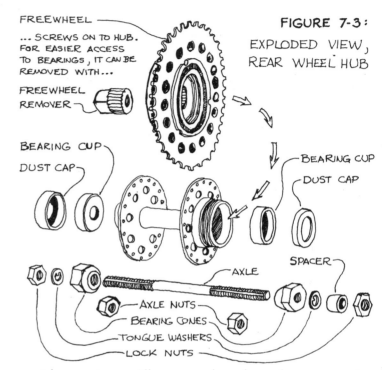

FIGURE 7-3:
EXPLODED VIEW, REAR WHEEL HUB

FREEWHEEL — ... SCREWS ON TO HUB. FOR EASIER ACCESS TO BEARINGS, IT CAN BE REMOVED WITH ...

FREEWHEEL REMOVER

BEARING CUP
DUST CAP

BEARING CUP
DUST CAP

AXLE
SPACER

AXLE NUTS
BEARING CONES
TONGUE WASHERS
LOCK NUTS

apart by amateurs. All you need to do to keep yours in shape is to give it a monthly oiling as prescribed in Chapter 5. These mechanisms are fairly fool-proof, but they are complicated: see Figure 7-4 if you don't believe it. So lubricate your hub from the outside, and don't try to disassemble it—you might never get it back together again. Once a year—or maybe once every two years if you keep your bike well lubricated in the interim—you should have your serviceman tear apart the hub and re-lubricate it for you.

Derailleur-equipped rear wheel hubs come apart and go together much the same as front wheel hubs. The main added complications are these:

(1) You have to take the chain off the rear sprocket cluster before you can remove the wheel. You don't have to pull the chain apart to get it off for this operation; just position the speed control levers so the chain is on the smallest chainwheel and rear sprocket, and "derail" the chain with your fingers. Then slip the wheel out of the frame slots.

(2) As you are removing the wheel, note very carefully the position of all spacers and washers, and make sure they go back on the same way you took them off. This will help insure that the rear sprocket cluster is properly lined up with the chainwheel.

(3) To disassemble the hub, it is easiest to clamp the wheel in a vise, sprocket-side down, gripping the locknut on the sprocket cluster side in the vise jaws.

(4) Working from the top, take off the other locknut, washer, and adjustable bearing cone. Then, holding the wheel by the axle (to keep the axle from slipping out

the bottom of the hub), loosen the vise and move the whole assembly to a clean newspaper laid out on the floor. Remove the axle and bearings.

The cleaning, inspection, relubrication, and reassembly can then proceed just as for the front hub.

CHAIN

The simple lubricating routine mentioned in Chapter 5 will go a long way toward keeping your chain from an early grave. But every 200 miles or so (more often if you ride around dusty places a lot), you should remove the chain, soak it in kerosene, and relubricate it with a light oil or silicone lubricant. Even when you remove the back wheel, you'll find the chain is still looped through the frame. To get it completely free of the bike, you must unlink the loop.

There are different ways to get the chain off, depending on what type of bike you have. Internally

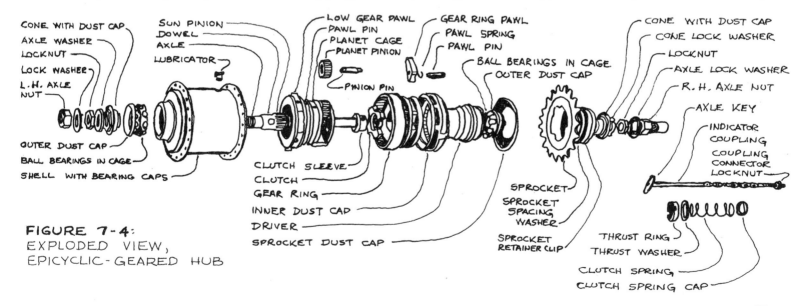

FIGURE 7-4:
EXPLODED VIEW,
EPICYCLIC-GEARED HUB

geared and simple coaster brake bikes have one type of chain while derailleur-equipped bikes have a different type of chain.

Chains on epicyclic-geared and coaster brake bikes use a master locking link (see Figure 7-5). To remove the chain, you simply remove the master link. This is easy to do if you have a thin screwdriver. Insert the blade under the removable side piece and *gently* pry out and up. Don't pry too hard or you'll break or bend the link out of shape. If you have the type of master link with a split end, spread the link apart slightly with thin-nosed pliers or a screwdriver. When half of the link is loose, swing it to one side and slide it off the grooved pin. Then disengage the rest of the link and the chain comes apart. Clean the master link and set it aside with all its pieces in order.

The chain on a derailleur-equipped bike usually has no master link. (If yours has one, its permanent removal is recommended—a master link can rub on the rear sprockets, causing premature wear and the possibility of derailleur malfunction.) To get a no-master-link chain off, and back on, you will need a rivet removing and installing tool (see Figure 6-2). Press the chain rivet part way out with the tool, then remove the tool and pry the chain apart with a screwdriver. Try to leave the rivet end showing slightly inside the chain link. This will make it easier to pop the rivet back into the link hole when you reassemble the chain later on.

If you decide to use a good old-fashioned oil instead of silicone as your chain lubricant, keep some light oil in a flat tin—such as a rectangular cake tin. You can keep dust and dirt out by covering it with plastic wrap. When you get the chain off the bike, first wipe it as clean as you can with paper towels. Then dunk it in kerosene to get it really clean, and wipe with more pa-

per towels or rags. Then drop it into the tin of oil and let it sit for a while (say 15 minutes) to allow the oil to soak in. Finally, remove the chain from the oil, wipe the excess away, and reinstall the chain on your bike. (While you have the chain off, you should consider removing and regreasing the crank bearings, since that job requires removal of the chain anyway. See below.)

Don't throw out the leftover oil after you've finished soaking the chain. Keep it. As long as you clean the chain first before dipping it into the oil, and keep the oil dirt-free between uses, it will last practically indefinitely.

If you like to experiment with things that are new, try silicone lubricant on your chain. Use kerosene to get all traces of oil off the chain and sprockets. Then replace the chain on the bike and spray on the silicone lubricant, which comes in an aerosol can. Use a thin plastic tube that fits over the spray nozzle (it usually comes with the can) to direct the stream of lubricant onto the joints of the chain. Wipe off any excess—a little goes a long way.

SNAP-ON TYPE.

SPLIT LINK

SPRING-CONNECTED TYPE.

FIGURE 7-5: CHAIN MASTER LINK

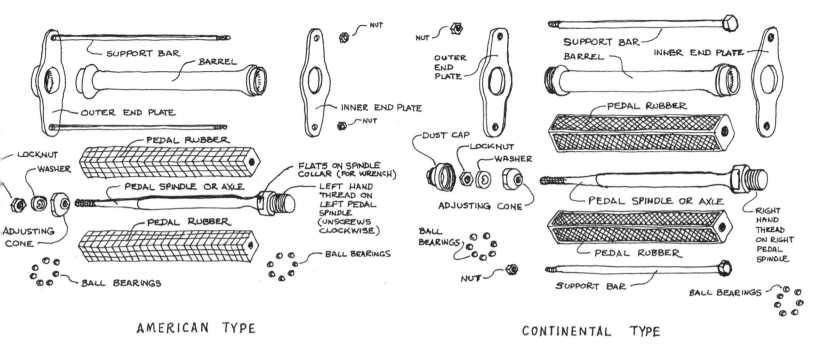

FIGURE 7-6: EXPLODED VIEW — AMERICAN AND CONTINENTAL PEDAL ASSEMBLIES

PEDALS

Because they are close to the ground, pedals pick up a lot of dust and—if you ride through puddles—moisture. So they need regreasing at least once a year; twice a year or more if you use your bike a lot. To do the regreasing, you will have to take the pedals apart. Here is how you do it:

(1) Remove the pedals from the crank. To do this, you will need to know that the left pedal spindle has a left-hand thread. This means it unscrews clockwise, which is opposite to the way a normal screw works. The right pedal spindle has a normal, right-hand thread, and unscrews in the regular counterclockwise way.

There are many different kinds of pedal assemblies, but they can be grouped into two basic types: American and Continental. Both are shown exploded in Figure 7-6. The main difference is that the Continental type usually has a removable dust cap at the outside end of the pedal spindle and the American type does not. On the American type, the outside section is in one piece and you have to take the inner pedal rubber end plate off to get at the bearings.

(2) If you have American-type pedals, proceed as follows: Remove the two small nuts at the threaded end of the pedal spindle; pull out the inner end plate; and remove the spindle assembly.

If you have Continental-type pedals, all you have to do to get to the same point is to remove the dust cap covering the outer end of the pedal spindle. The remaining routine is the same for both types of pedals.

(3) Remove the locknut, washer, and the adjustable cone. Do this job over a rag laid on the ground or workbench to catch the ball bearings if they are loose. If the bearings are loose, count them before or as you remove them, and make sure they all go back in when you reassemble. If the bearings are in cages, note the way the wider side of the cage faces the cone, and the smaller side faces the cup.

(4) Remove the bearings. If they are in cages, lay the cages out in the order and direction in which they are removed.

(5) Clean the bearings, cups, and cones in kerosene, and dry with a clean cloth.

(6) Check all parts, including the pedal rubbers, for wear. Replace any parts that look worn.

(7) Smear some grease in the pedal cups.

(8) Put the whole works back together. When you screw on the adjustable cone, turn it down snugly by hand (until the pedal begins to bind slightly), then back it off a quarter turn. The pedal should now spin freely, but shouldn't be loose enough for side play.

CRANK BEARINGS

Crank bearings (also called "hanger set," "crank hanger bearings," or "bottom bracket bearings") need disassembly for greasing once a year. Usually greasing

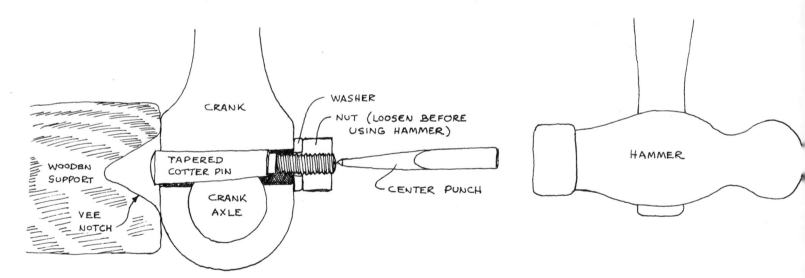

FIGURE 7-7: REMOVING COTTER PIN FROM COTTERED CRANK

is the only method of lubrication used. However, occasionally you will find a bike with an oil hole or oil cup on top of the bottom bracket. If you see an oil hole or cup, give it a squirt of light oil once a month, in addition to the annual complete relubrication.

To get at some types of crank bearings, you will have to take off at least one pedal. A good move is to take off both pedals and regrease them at the same time you regrease the crank bearings. (See the procedures on pedal removal and lubrication above.)

Crank assemblies come in three different styles: "one-piece," "three-piece cottered," and "three-piece cotterless." Disassembly routines are different for each type. Most American-made bikes use a one-piece forging that includes both cranks; the crank bearings are usually in cages. European styles, on the other hand, usually have removable cranks, either held in by heavy, tapered cotter pins (cottered type), or kept in position by square ends on the crank axle mating with square holes on the crank arms (cotterless type). European-style crank bearings are usually loose (not in cages).

One-piece cranks.

(1) Remove the chainguard, chain, and left pedal. Remember that the left pedal unscrews clockwise.

(2) With an open-end wrench, loosen the locknut on the left side of the bottom bracket and slip it off the end of the crank. Then slip off the other parts you will find underneath: a key washer, dust cap, adjustable bearing cone, and ball bearing cage and bearings.

(3) Then wiggle the entire crank assembly out through the right side of the bottom bracket.

(4) Clean, lubricate, and reassemble. Use an all-purpose grease, such as Lubriplate Type A.

Three-piece cottered crank assemblies.

(1) Remove the chainguard and chain.

(2) Remove the tapered cotter pin on each crank arm. This is a little tricky. Loosen the nuts on the pins. To get the tapered pins loose in their tapered holes, you'll have to push them out one way or another. There are several recommended ways to do this. One way is to press them out with a C-clamp. This is a good method to use if you can find a way to keep the C-clamp from slipping when you start to tighten it. Using a wheel-puller instead of a C-clamp may be possible, if you have one. Tapping the loosened nut with a hammer is another possibility—but you run the risk of damaging the threads on the nut or the pin, and if you hammer too vigorously you might bend the pin. Using the hammer to tap a center punch carefully against the very center of the tapered pin will help avoid thread damage, but you still may bend the pin if you hit too hard. In any case, if you decide to loosen the pin by hitting it with a hammer instead of squeezing it loose with a clamp or wheel-puller, support the crank axle on a wooden support with a Vee notch. (see Figure 7-7). Otherwise you may bend the crank axle.

(3) When you take a pin out, note the direction the flat side faces so you can put it back in the same way later.

(4) Slip off the crank arms.

(5) Loosen the locking ring on the left side of the bottom bracket, using the large moon-shaped part of your pressed-steel bicycle wrench (Figure 6-1), and remove it, along with the left bearing cup and ball bearings. Catch the loose ball bearings on a newspaper or a cloth spread out on the ground under the bottom bracket. Your best bet to keep the bearings from getting away from you is to lay the bike on its side for this step. Be careful not to lose any bearings up into the frame tubes, the holes of which open into the bottom bracket.

(6) Withdraw the crank axle.

(7) Clean, lubricate, and reassemble.

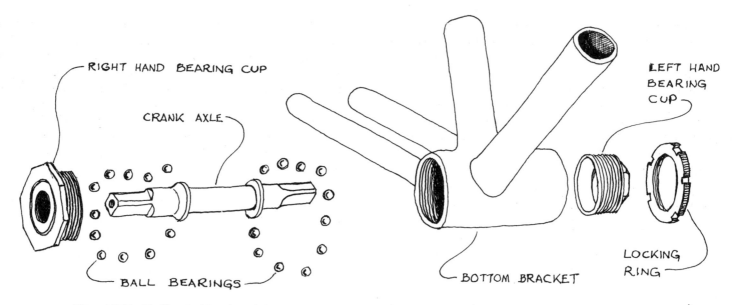

FIGURE 7-8: TYPICAL CRANK BEARING ASSEMBLY (THREE-PIECE COTTERLESS TYPE)

Three-piece cotterless cranks. The procedure with these varies depending on the particular make of bike, and you may need some special tools to do the job. Generally the procedure goes like this:

(1) Remove the chainguard and chain.

(2) Remove the dust caps at each end of the crank axle. You may need a special tool made for your particular crank assembly—or if you are lucky, you can improvise with an adjustable open-end wrench, pliers, or other standard tools.

(3) Remove the crank nuts or screws exposed when you took off the dust caps. Again you may need a special tool (such as the TA Professional Crank Spanner in Figure 6-3) or you may be able to improvise.

(4) Pull the cranks off the axle. Here you need

another special tool: an extractor such as the one shown in Figure 6-3. This time you probably *shouldn't* try to improvise; instead, buy or borrow one. The main reason for extra care is that cotterless cranks are usually made of a soft alloy, such as duraluminum, which is more subject to damage than plain steel.

(5) Remove the bearings and axle in the same way as described for cottered-type crank assemblies.

(6) Clean, lubricate, and reassemble.

FRONT FORK BEARINGS

Like crank bearings, front fork bearings (sometimes called headset bearings) should be taken out and regreased once a year. Also like crank bearings, the American-made types usually have ball bearings in a cage, whereas the European types are loose. Here's the routine for disassembly:

(1) Get the front wheel brake assembly out of the way. This means that if you have side-pull caliper brakes, you'll need to remove the front brake. This is easy: just unscrew the nut at the rear of the fork and remove the entire brake assembly. You don't have to remove the brake assembly if you have center-pull brakes. Just remove the short horizontal cable that connects the brake yoke to the vertical brake cable.

(2) Unscrew the expander bolt on top of the handlebar stem about ¼ inch.

(3) Tap the loosened bolt with a hammer, using a block of wood between the hammer and the bolt head to prevent damage to the bolt head.

(4) Grab the handlebars and twist and pull upward, keeping the front fork and wheel under control by squeezing them between your knees. Pull the handlebar and stem assembly all the way out and set it aside.

(5) Remove the locknut at the top of the steering head. If it is a hex nut, use a large open-end wrench, a crescent wrench, or your trusty bicycle wrench. If it is a round, washer-like affair with small holes around the edge, use a pipe-wrench, a special wrench made for the purpose, or tap the sides of the holes in the direction the nut unscrews with a center punch and hammer. Be careful not to damage the holes.

(6) Remove the front wheel.

(7) Lay the bicycle on its side with newspaper or cloth spread out underneath to catch parts, then remove the keyed washer and adjustable bearing cup from the top of the steering head.

(8) Pull the fork out from the bottom of the steering head. Pick out any loose ball bearings that didn't already drop out from either the top or the bottom of

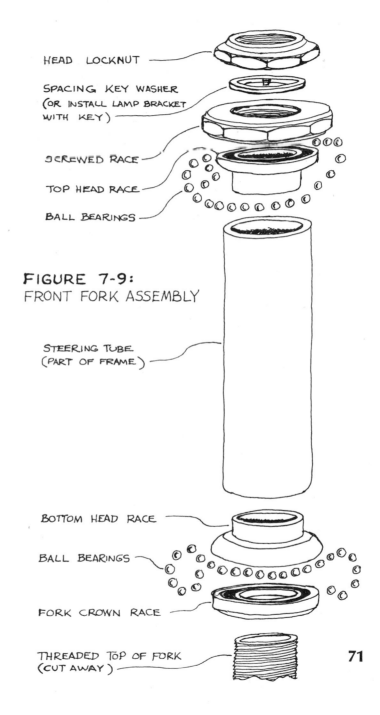

FIGURE 7-9:
FRONT FORK ASSEMBLY

HEAD LOCKNUT

SPACING KEY WASHER (OR INSTALL LAMP BRACKET WITH KEY)

SCREWED RACE

TOP HEAD RACE

BALL BEARINGS

STEERING TUBE (PART OF FRAME)

BOTTOM HEAD RACE

BALL BEARINGS

FORK CROWN RACE

THREADED TOP OF FORK (CUT AWAY)

71

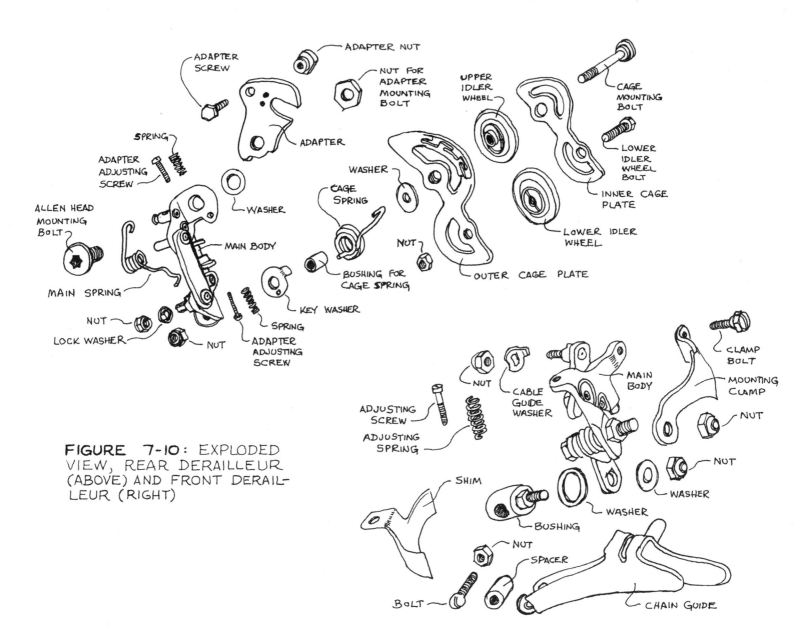

ADAPTER SCREW

ADAPTER NUT

NUT FOR ADAPTER MOUNTING BOLT

UPPER IDLER WHEEL

CAGE MOUNTING BOLT

SPRING

ADAPTER ADJUSTING SCREW

ADAPTER

LOWER IDLER WHEEL BOLT

INNER CAGE PLATE

ALLEN HEAD MOUNTING BOLT

WASHER

WASHER

CAGE SPRING

LOWER IDLER WHEEL

MAIN BODY

MAIN SPRING

NUT

BUSHING FOR CAGE SPRING

OUTER CAGE PLATE

NUT

LOCK WASHER

NUT

KEY WASHER

SPRING

ADAPTER ADJUSTING SCREW

FIGURE 7-10: EXPLODED VIEW, REAR DERAILLEUR (ABOVE) AND FRONT DERAILLEUR (RIGHT)

NUT

CABLE GUIDE WASHER

MAIN BODY

CLAMP BOLT

MOUNTING CLAMP

ADJUSTING SCREW

ADJUSTING SPRING

NUT

NUT

WASHER

SHIM

BUSHING

WASHER

NUT

SPACER

BOLT

CHAIN GUIDE

72

the steering head, and be careful not to lose any up inside the frame tubes.

(9) Clean and regrease with Lubriplate Type A or similar grease.

(10) To start reassembly, turn the bike upside down. Smear grease in the bottom cone, replace the bearings, and insert the front fork. Then you can turn the bike right side up again, holding the front fork in place to keep the bottom bearings where they belong.

(11) Finish reassembly, adjusting the bearing cones so that the front fork neither binds nor feels too loose—and the job is done.

The only mechanisms left to discuss which need lubrication are the front and rear derailleur mechanisms, and the freewheel mechanism found inside the rear gear cluster on derailleur-equipped bikes. So, unless you have a derailleur bike, you've finished the lubri-cation exercise if you've done everything described above.

FREEWHEEL AND DERAILLEUR MECHANISMS

I recommend you don't disassemble either the freewheel or the derailleur mechanisms to lubricate them; they are easy to get out of adjustment and, besides, the freewheel needs a special tool to get it off. So every 30 days or so, just put a few drops of light oil into the freewheel mechanism, and onto the moving parts of the front and rear derailleurs and gearshift levers. Every year or two, if you trust your friendly bike repairman, let *him* pull these mechanisms apart. If you want to know what your derailleurs look like in pieces, watch the repairman when he works on your bike—or look at Figure 7-10.

That's all there is to lubricating your bike, more or less. Next let's consider some repairs you can make.

8

REPAIRS YOU CAN MAKE

Obscure as well as obvious things can go wrong with your bike. This chapter describes a few of the more common problems, and explains what you can do about them.

TIRE TROUBLES

Bike tires can go flat for a number of reasons. The trouble may start with a leaky valve core or a cracked or broken valve stem. Tube leakage, which is a more common problem, is caused by old age and cracked rubber, overflexing resulting from underinflation, rupture resulting from overinflation, rough usage (such as running over curbs or overloading the bike), or running over glass or sharp stones.

Tire trouble can be minimized, if not prevented, by following the simple suggestions in the chapter on basic care of your bike. But you may have a flat even when you try to follow all the rules. To repair it, here's what to do:

(1) First check to be sure it's not just a loose valve core. Remove the valve cap, inflate the tire to normal pressure, and put a little soapy water inside the valve.

If bubbles form, there's your problem. Try tightening the valve core, using the slotted valve cap to turn it (clockwise to tighten, counterclockwise to loosen). If this doesn't stop the bubbles, install a new core.

(2) If the leak isn't at the core, the next step is to remove the wheel. While it's possible to fix a leaky tube without dismantling the wheel, it's usually easier to take the wheel off to do it. Chapter 7 tells about wheel removal.

(3) Completely deflate the tube by unscrewing the core all the way.

(4) Remove the tire from the rim. You should try to do this without tools—it's too easy to damage a tube or tire with the sharp end of a screwdriver or other prying tool stuck between the tire and rim. If you *must* use tools to pry the tire away from the rim, don't use anything sharp. You can get bicycle tire irons that are designed for the job (see Figure 6-3)—or you can use a couple of regular tablespoons. Here is how to do the job with your bare hands.

Stand the wheel upright on the ground and, gripping the tire at the top, push down, forcing the tire beads into the rim. Then slide your hands around and down along the tire towards the floor, pulling the tire around so the part at the top of the wheel is forced tightly against the rim and the bottom part is pushed away from the rim. When your hands get about halfway around from top to bottom, lift the wheel from the floor. Continue pulling the tire toward the bottom of the wheel. When your hands are almost together, roll the tire off the rim. The tube will come with it.

Sometimes spraying a little silicone on the wheel rim will help in rolling and sliding the tire over the rim edge. (Silicone won't hurt rubber; oil will. *Never* use oil on the rim.)

(5) Examine the tube and find the puncture. If you don't see any hole, pump up the tube and dip it in a bucket of water, immersing part at a time. You'll see bubbles coming from the point of puncture.

(6) Repair the puncture, using a patch kit. (Instructions are usually enclosed with the kit.) If the tube is old, or you don't want to take any chances on your patching skills, or if the break in the tire is too big to patch, replace the tube with a new one.

(7) See if you can find the cause of the puncture. This means checking the inside of the tire to make sure there are no nails or other sharp objects sticking through that will cause another puncture later on. First examine the inside of the tire by eye, using a flashlight. Then run your fingers around the inside wall, feeling for bumps or sharp points. If you find any, remove them.

(8) Check the rim for dents, rust, or loose or rough spoke heads.

(9) Make sure the protective strip around the inside of the rim is smoothly laid down and covers all spoke heads.

(10) Dust the tube with talcum powder to make it easier to get it back on the rim without pinching or binding.

(11) Inflate the tube a little until it starts to regain its shape. Stuff it back into the loose tire, and smooth it down so it's not twisted, wrinkled, or pinched.

(12) Insert the valve stem into the valve hole in the rim.

(13) Starting at the valve, with one hand on each side of the wheel, push one beaded edge of the tire onto the rim. Go all the way around the edge until one bead is all the way on. Then push the other bead on in the same way.

(14) With the tire on the rim but not yet fully inflated, bounce the wheel a couple of times against the

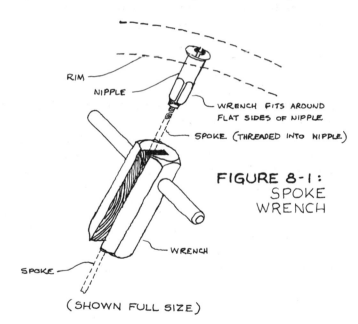

RIM
NIPPLE
WRENCH FITS AROUND FLAT SIDES OF NIPPLE
SPOKE (THREADED INTO NIPPLE)

FIGURE 8-1: SPOKE WRENCH

WRENCH
SPOKE

(SHOWN FULL SIZE)

ground to work out any wrinkles or pinched spots in the tube that may have formed.

(15) Inflate the tire to about ten pounds pressure. Check to make sure both beads are properly seated on the rim.

(16) Deflate the tire again for more insurance against a pinched or binding tube.

(17) Repeat inflation to ten pounds, and check rim seating again. Check also to be sure that the valve stem is not bent as it emerges from the valve hole.

(18) Inflate to full pressure. See Chapter 5 for tips on how to keep the tire from exploding in your face.

(19) Replace the wheel on the bike, and you're finished.

Note on high pressure leaks. Sometimes a tube will develop a mysterious malady known as a "high pressure leak." When you pump up the tube inside the tire, it will go flat within a few hours or days, but when you remove the tube from the tire, put some air in it and check for leaks, you won't be able to find any. The reason is that, when it's outside the tire, the tube will only hold about five pounds of pressure before swelling dangerously out of shape. But at only five pounds pressure, air can't force its way out through the tiny hole that's causing the leak. If you have a tube with a high pressure leak, it is difficult or impossible to find the spot to patch it. Your best bet is to throw the leaky tube away and buy a new one.

Flat tires (sewn-type). Because most of the readers of this book will be using clincher tires on their bikes rather than the thin-walled, lightweight sewn type sometimes used on racing bikes, the rather complicated procedure for repairing a sewn-type tire will not be described here. However, if your bike has sewn-type tires that need repair, comprehensive descriptions of the removal, patching, sewing, and gluing that you'll need to do are given in several of the books listed in the Bibliography. Or, you can always take the wheel to your repairman.

Loose spokes. If you have a lot of loose spokes, or if your wheels wobble noticeably when you spin them, you should probably have your wheels trued up by a serviceman. But if only one or two spokes are a little loose, it's an easy job to adjust them to proper tightness. To do the job you'll need a spoke wrench. Here's the procedure:

(1) Turn over your bike so it rests on the ground on its saddle and handlebars.

(2) Spin the wheel to be adjusted, holding an object (like the spoke wrench) lightly against the moving spokes. You will hear a series of "pings."

(3) Listen to the pings. They should all be at the same musical pitch. If some of the spokes go "ping" and others go "clunk"—that is, they make a lower-pitched sound—the "clunkers" need tightening. Figure 8-1 shows how you do it.

BRAKE TROUBLES

Coaster brakes. If you have coaster brakes on your bike, they should function properly for several years before wearing enough to need major adjustment. If your coaster brakes are not working properly, take the bike to a repairman. Don't try to fix it yourself; the insides of a coaster brake hub are too complicated.

Caliper brakes. If you have caliper brakes—the kind with rubber pads or "shoes" that squeeze down on the wheel rims when you operate a lever or levers mounted on the handlebars—examine the pads. If they look worn, or are old, hard, shiny, and have lost their rubbery friction, you should replace them. It's easy.

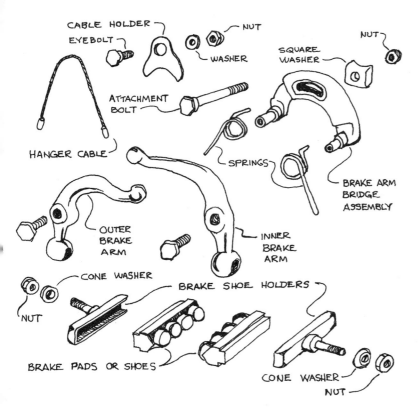

CABLE HOLDER
EYEBOLT
NUT
WASHER
SQUARE WASHER
NUT
ATTACHMENT BOLT
HANGER CABLE
SPRINGS
BRAKE ARM BRIDGE ASSEMBLY
OUTER BRAKE ARM
INNER BRAKE ARM
CONE WASHER
NUT
BRAKE SHOE HOLDERS
BRAKE PADS OR SHOES
CONE WASHER
NUT

FIGURE 8-2 : EXPLODED VIEW, TYPICAL CALIPER BRAKES

(1) With the proper wrench, unscrew the nuts holding the brake blocks on the brake arms (see Figure 8-2).

(2) Spread the brake arms apart, and pull out the blocks and the rubber pads.

(3) Replace them with new ones. (Some pads are permanently attached to their metal "blocks" or holders, others are removable. It's a good idea to buy new metal holders along with the rubber pads; the holders cost only a few pennies more, and they're apt to be deteriorating anyway by the time the rubber pads wear out.)

(4) When reattaching the blocks, be sure that the open ends are toward the rear so the pads don't slip out along the wheel rim when the brakes are applied. Also, be careful to adjust the pads so their surfaces line up exactly with the surface of the wheel rim. Don't let the pads rub against the tire—they will wear out the tire sidewalls in no time.

When adjusting the caliper brakes, the rubber pads should each be about ⅛ inch away from the wheel when the brake control lever is released. If they are too close or too far away from the rim, you will get the feeling that they are too "tight" or "loose" when squeezing the brake lever. On some types of brakes (the more expensive ones), you can adjust the pads in toward the wheel by turning an adjustment screw or nut right at the brake block. On other types, you adjust the brake cable instead by loosening the locknut on an adjusting barrel and turning the barrel (see Figure 2-10).

Caliper brake cable. If the brake cable has stretched so you can no longer take up the slack by turning the adjusting barrel, you can usually adjust it by loosening the anchor nut that holds the cable end in place (to the cable holder on center-pull brakes, or to the brake arm on side-pull brakes), and pulling the cable through a little more.

If your brake cable breaks and requires replacement, take the old one into the bike shop with you to make sure the replacement is the same length and thickness, and has the same type of ends. (Some cables have two special leaded ends, others are plain on one end and leaded on the other.) To get the cable off, assuming it's frayed but not broken, loosen the end at the wheel and pull the cable out through the control lever, helping it along by pushing up from underneath. Note how the upper cable end is held in place. When you put the new cable in, use the same procedure you used to take the old one out, in reverse.

Squealing caliper brakes. Squealing may be induced by old, worn, or hardened rubber brake pads. If this turns out to be the cause of your problem, simply replace the pads. If it's not, check the brake arms and the rest of the mechanism for tightness. Squealing can result from the vibration of loose parts. If everything is tight, check the pads to make sure they're clean; particles of grit embedded in the rubber may also cause squealing.

Another reason for squealing caliper brakes could be the angle at which the brake shoe meets the rim. If this seems to be your trouble, bend the arm that holds the offending brake shoe so the front side of the shoe turns in. Use a crescent wrench or offset pliers to hold the arm firmly as you bend it.

GEAR TROUBLES

There are so many different kinds of derailleurs and gear hubs, each with their own adjustment techniques, that I'm not going to attempt to describe any of them here. Such adjustments are usually simple and quick for somebody who knows what he is doing, but can be disastrous for the uninformed. If you think your shift mechanism needs adjustment, I recommend you take your bike to a repair expert. It will be quicker, and maybe even cheaper, than trying to figure out how to do it yourself.

OTHER TROUBLES

The list of things that can go wrong with bikes could go on and on. What you see here is just a sample— but it covers most of the major problems. If your bike has trouble that you don't think is covered here, you may be able to figure out how to fix it by using the following techniques:

Try to isolate the problem. If it is a squeaking or grinding noise, turn the bike upside down and work the pedals, shift the gears, and spin the wheels. Keep looking and listening. Look especially for parts rubbing where they are not supposed to (such as the chainguard rubbing against the chain, or a fender rubbing against a tire).

Study the problem and decide what to do. If it's a rubbing fender or chainguard, the decision on what to do is easy: gently bend the out-of-place part back into its correct position. But if it's a noise coming from inside the front hub, for example, you should study the pictures and text in Chapter 7 which describes what's inside the front hub. Then you can decide whether to take it apart, relubricate it, and hope that fixes the trouble, or whether to restudy the symptom and perhaps decide on another course of action.

Take appropriate action. Don't ignore strange noises or any other symptoms that seem to indicate there's something wrong with your bike. *Do something about the problem.* What could be a simple matter of squirting a few drops of oil here or there can grow into a potentially expensive replacement job if action isn't taken as soon as the symptom is recognized. And if you can't figure out what to do about your bike's symptoms, take it to somebody who can (like your friendly bike repairman).

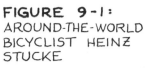

FIGURE 9-1:
AROUND-THE-WORLD
BICYCLIST HEINZ
STUCKE

HAVING FUN

You have looked at different styles of bikes, new and used, and chosen one. You've learned to ride it competently and safely, and have shined, polished, and oiled it, taken it apart and put it back together again, adjusted and repaired it. You've loaded it with accessories for convenience, or stripped it of accessories for speed. In doing all these things, you've learned what bikes and bicycling are all about: having fun! In this chapter, let's look at some other ways you can have fun with them.

DECORATING YOUR BIKE

You can get quite a variety of decorative materials especially designed for bikes. You can also improvise, using commonly available materials. Figure 9-2 shows a typical result of somebody's urge to dress up a bike. If you have such an urge, let your creativity soar!

Especially designed for bike use are such inspired beautification aids as bike baskets with plastic flowers attached; plastic tubes for decorating spokes; colored wheel disks (see Figure 9-3 for some typical designs) and colored sidewall tires; splash flaps for rear fenders; handlebar clamp-ons for attaching such doodads as miniature American flags, plastic animals, or plastic pin-wheels that spin in the wind; bike paint in matching colors (or almost any other color you can think of) in either spray or brush-on type; and flowered or psychedelic-design saddles.

Other material available at your nearest variety store includes:

Colored plastic tape. This is great for making rally stripes, candy stripes, or jailbird stripes. Instead of just plain plastic tape, you can use reflective tape for some weird nighttime effects (and it also makes a safer bike).

Plastic adhesive-backed numbers. These give a racing car effect. (From a more practical standpoint, bike numbers clearly visible from a distance are useful

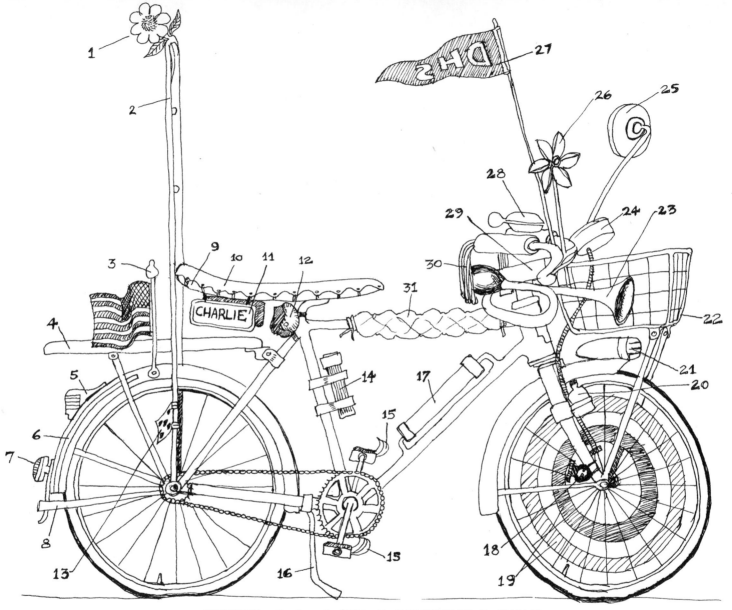

FIGURE 9-2: A "FULLY EQUIPPED" BICYCLE
(FOR LOCAL ROADS ONLY)

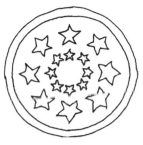

FIGURE 9-3 : COLORED WHEEL DISK DESIGNS

KEY TO FIGURE 9-2

1. PLASTIC FLOWER
2. ROLL BAR
3. FLAG AND STAFF
4. LUGGAGE RACK
5. TAILLIGHT
6. REFLECTIVE TAPE
7. REFLECTOR
8. KICKSTAND, REAR TYPE
9. BANANA SEAT
10. SEAT COVER
11. "LICENSE PLATE" TYPE SIGN
12. TOOL KIT
13. PLAYING CARD "MOTOR"
14. FLASHLIGHT AND SNAP-IN HOLDER
15. TOE CLIPS
16. KICKSTAND, SIDE TYPE
17. AIR PUMP
18. CYCLOMETER
19. DECORATIVE CREPE PAPER
20. ELECTRIC GENERATOR
21. HEADLIGHT
22. BASKET
23. HORN
24. SPEEDOMETER
25. REAR VIEW MIRROR
26. PINWHEEL
27. SCHOOL PENNANT ON RADIO AERIAL
28. BELL
29. BIKE RADIO
30. HANDLEBAR GRIP TASSLES
31. PADDING FOR PASSENGER COMFORT

in certain games, such as bike polo.) A wooden, plastic, or paper panel tied to the top, bottom, and seat tubes with string, wire, or tape, makes an effective background for the number. (For temporary use, try a paper plate.)

Plastic adhesive-backed designs. Stick them (flowers, symbols, mottos, etc.) on fenders, saddles, or panels you can make to display them.

Crepe paper. Try using colored crepe paper to decorate your wheels. You can weave strips through your spokes in concentric circles, taping the ends to hold the works together. But you'll need to keep the crepe paper from getting wet. If it gets wet, it will disintegrate, and you'll be left with a mass of pulpy, wet paper scraps.

Playing-card motor. Is it a decoration? You could call it "decorative sound," although some adults might call it "noise pollution" instead. All you need is a spring clothespin and one playing card (take one from an incomplete deck of cards, rather than spoiling a full deck by removing a card). Clamp the card onto a frame tube or fender support so the tip of the card is sticking between the spokes. (See Figure 9-4.) When you ride, the card will make a snapping sound, vaguely like the sound of a motorcycle engine.

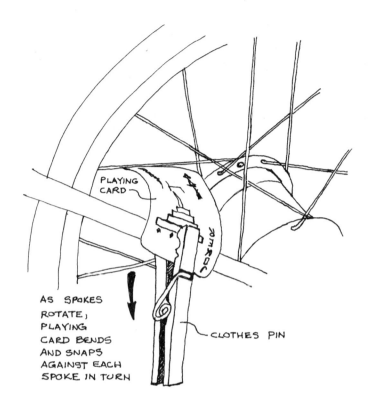

PLAYING
CARD

AS SPOKES
ROTATE,
PLAYING
CARD BENDS
AND SNAPS
AGAINST EACH
SPOKE IN TURN

—— CLOTHES PIN

FIGURE 9-4: PLAYING CARD MOTOR

GAMES BICYCLISTS PLAY

There are lots of games you can play on bikes. Some test your riding skills, some test your stamina, and some, like bike polo, are a combined test of riding skill, stamina, and overall physical prowess. All are fun (some more so for kids than adults), and most can be practiced either in groups or by yourself. This section devotes attention to just a few of the principal games played to give you an idea of the possibilities.

Slalom race. In the slalom race, the cyclist follows a course marked by two parallel zigzag chalk or string lines on a road or field. The lines should be about five feet apart, with each straight section being about 20 feet long. Each turn should be about 110 degrees, or a little more than a right angle. It's a good idea to set up at least four or five turns, and up to a dozen or more if you have the space. Buckets, stones, or other markers at each turn help to orient the rider to the course he has to follow. Start and finish lines are at opposite ends of the course, and should be well marked. Each rider is timed as he races through the course, and the shortest time wins. The rider is disqualified if his bike touches any of the lines or markers, or if either of his feet touches the ground.

Spiral race. The spiral race is sort of a right-turn-only slalom race. A line (chalk or string), which spirals inward and leaves a path about four feet wide which terminates at a dead-end in the center, constitutes the course. Each contestant winds his way clockwise inward along the spiral path. He is disqualified for crossing the line at any point, or for touching the ground with either foot before reaching the center. The fastest time wins.

Snail race. Here the object is to pedal a straight course between start and finish as *slowly* as possible. Several lanes four or five feet wide should be laid out, using string or chalk. A rider is disqualified for crossing into another lane, turning his bike around, or touching a foot to the ground. All the contestants start at once on a signal. The last one to finish wins.

Coasting race. In a coasting race, each rider starts separately at a starting line, 15 or more feet behind a "stop-pedalling line." He pedals as fast as he can until he reaches the stop-pedalling line, then coasts until his bike slows up to the point where he can no longer balance. A referee marks the spot where he stops. The rider who gets his bike to coast the farthest beyond the stop-pedalling line wins.

Distance racing. Organized amateur bike racing is sponsored in the U.S.A. and Canada by the Amateur Bicycle League of America (P.O. Box 2175, New York, New York 10017). You can contact them for particulars if you take your racing seriously. The Bicycle Institute of America (122 East 42nd Street, New York, New York 10017) also has some free helpful literature on bike racing. Or you can organize your own races informally. Choose any distance. Straight sprint races of 50, 100, or 150 yards are convenient if you're using an athletic field as your race course. You can do laps around the running track if it has one. Or road race for anywhere from ¼ mile to 5, 10, 50, or 100 miles. If you feel like riding 100 miles, though, I suggest you first get in touch with the League of American Wheelmen, (5118 Foster Avenue, Chicago, Illinois 60630). They conduct what they call a "Century Run" (since it's 100 miles), and give away pins as awards for riders who successfully complete the 100-mile run. You might as well get something for your effort. But to qualify for the pin, you have to finish in a maximum of 12 hours (though you can stop to rest occasionally if you want to; you don't have to ride continuously).

In Europe, where bicycling both as a basic means of transportation and as a sport has progressed much further than in the United States or Canada, professional and amateur races are run regularly. All Europe watches the annual Tour de France, an over-the-mountains bike race that lasts several days and generates the same high pitch of spectator excitement as professional football does in the U.S.

Bicycle polo. Bicycle polo (also called "bike polo" in the U.S. and "cycle polo" in Europe) is a great game if you can find eight people with bikes, a field to play on, and are willing to acquire a few items of equipment. You should have a regulation polo ball and a set of polo mallets with cut-down (30-inch) shafts. If you don't want to invest in such fancy stuff, you can try substituting a wooden croquet ball and croquet mallets, although these are not particularly suitable. The handles on croquet mallets are slightly shorter than they should be for regulation bike polo. Short mallets make it more difficult to hit the ball.

The rules of bicycle polo and regular horse polo are basically the same. Two teams of four bikes each try to drive a ball through goal posts placed 12 feet apart at opposite ends of a field. The field dimensions are set at 110 by 80 yards maximum, which is 1/3 the size of a regulation horse polo field. The only other significant differences between regular and bike polo are (1) that a bike polo player can't strike the ball more than three times in a row, and (2) that contact with other players or bikes is not allowed.

The field dimensions are flexible up to the stated maximum so you can use a football field if you happen to have one handy. Whatever the size, a center line and field boundaries need to be clearly marked. Here's a thumbnail summary of what goes on:

(1) Each team has four players: two forwards, who play an offensive game, and two backs, who act as defensive guards to keep the opponents from scoring.

(2) To start the game, the two teams line up para-

llel to the center line on their own side of the field and begin to circle counterclockwise as the referee, from the side line, starts a countdown from 10 to 0. At the call of "ZERO," the ball is rolled between the two groups of circling players.

(3) If the ball rolls out of bounds, the referee rolls it back into play at the point where it crossed the line, after counting down to zero again. No player should be closer to the line than five yards when the ball is rolled.

(4) No player may strike the ball when dismounted; even one foot touching the ground is considered "dismounted."

(5) A player may not "ride off" an opponent (i.e. push the opponent's bike out of the way with his own), or make contact in any way.

(6) A player may not catch or kick the ball, or hit it with anything except his stick.

(7) If there is a referee (as there usually is for serious play), he may call fouls and allow free drives (as in basketball).

(8) The game is customarily played in six five-minute periods and the team that scores the most goals wins.

If you really get serious about bike polo, you'll want to stock up on special equipment such as polo helmets, and maybe special T-shirts with your team's emblem emblazoned on the back and front. You may also consider acquiring a special bike for bike polo use. Some players prefer a minibike with 18- or 20-inch wheels because it gives them maneuverability. Others go

FIGURE 9-5:
BICYCLE POLO
PLAYERS IN
ACTION

84

for a stripped-down version of a touring bike. Its larger wheels and three-speed gears give superior speed, particularly useful on large fields.

Bicycle polo enthusiasts have developed some unique equipment that makes play more efficient and effective. One group even developed cut-down handlebars on their shot-making (right) side, so the sweep of the mallet would be less impeded. If you play a lot of bike polo, you'll no doubt come up with some equipment modifications of your own to make play easier, more efficient, or just more fun.

If you're interested in taking up the sport seriously, contact the U.S. Bicycle Polo Association (P.O. Box 565, FDR Station, New York, New York 10022).

There are plenty of other games besides those mentioned above. But the few outlined here should be enough to keep you occupied, at least for a while, if you are the game-playing type.

BIKEWAYS

One bicycling activity not mentioned elsewhere in this book is the growing use of bikeways. These are specially marked bicycle routes, paths, and trails. The first U.S. bikeway, called a "safety route," was opened in Homestead, Florida, in 1962. Since then, hundreds of cities, towns, and municipalities across the U.S.A. (and in many other countries, particularly in Europe, where the idea originated) have marked streets or constructed special paths leading from and to schools, recreation areas, and points of scenic or historic interest. Bikeways are well marked with signs (see Figure 9-6) not only to guide the bicyclist, but where the bikeway is also a regular roadway, to warn motorists that the route being followed has been designated to be shared with bicycles. Local, state, and federal government officials have

FIGURE 9-6:
BIKEWAY SIGNS

become increasingly interested in the principle of bikeways as the popularity of bicycling spreads. As a consequence new bike routes are being opened all the time. For example, Coral Gables, Florida, has more than 20 miles of marked "Bike Route," maintained by the city's Community Development Department. A network

FIGURE 9-7: HAVING FUN

of bikeways at the Cape Cod National Seashore, operated by the U.S. Department of the Interior, provides access to the various points of interest in that 27,000-acre park. An Ohio long-distance bikeway gives bicyclists an opportunity to tour the picturesque Amish countryside in relatively traffic-free peace. And New York City creates "instant bikeways" by closing Central Park roads to automobile traffic at designated times. As many as 10,000 bike-riding New Yorkers show up on warm Sunday afternoons to pedal through the car-free park.

Hundreds of other places already have bikeways, and hundreds more are on the way. If your community doesn't have any bikeways and you think they should, you personally may be able to do something about it. The Bicycle Institute of America (see address above) offers many ideas which can help you get a bikeway started in your area. They are free on request.

TOURING

If you're interested in touring on bikes with others, join the League of American Wheelmen (see address above). If you want to take a trip for a weekend or a week, American Youth Hostels (20 West 17th Street, New York, New York) has some free information you'll be interested in.

Touring is great fun, but each trip must be properly planned and prepared for, whether it's a two-day or two-week outing. Most important, both you and your bike must be in top shape, and you should have the right equipment and supplies. A note on weight though: don't go overboard on luggage. Try to strike a balance between keeping down the loaded weight of the bike and having enough supplies to be reasonably comfortable. And remember to distribute the weight with a bigger proportion over the back wheel than the front for easier pedalling and steering. Or, as suggested earlier, carry your luggage in a bike trailer.

Some suggestions for touring equipment are listed in the Appendix. Not all of these things are necessities. What you choose to take on your trip should depend on the length of the trip, the climate, and what you are interested in seeing and doing on the trip.

Touring by bike for a lot longer than "a weekend or a week" is possible, of course. The recordholder in this regard is probably Mr. Heinz Stucke, a German who has covered more than 60,000 miles in a tour he's taking around the world. So far he's been at it for ten years, and is still going strong.

That's all there is to the basics of bikes. If you want to learn more about bicycling—America's number one participation sport—read some of the books listed in the Bibliography. And above all: Have fun! Happy Bicycling!

APPENDIX

BIBLIOGRAPHY

Andersen, Jane H., and Vilardo, Frank J. *Bicycle Accidents to School Aged Children.* Chicago: National Safety Council (Report #169), 1969.

Baranet, Nancy Neiman. *The Turned Down Bar.* Philadelphia: Dorrance, 1964.

Bartleet, Horace Wilton. *Bartleet's Bicycle Book.* London: E.J. Burrow & Co., 1931.

Bauer, Fred. *How Many Hills to Hillsboro.* Old Tappan, New Jersey: Hewitt House, 1969.

Benedict, Raymond and Ruth. *Bicycling.* New York: A.S. Barnes, 1944.

Bowden, Kenneth, and Mathews, John. *Cycle Racing.* London: Temple Press Books, 1965.

Carter, Ernest Frank. *The Boys' Book of Cycles and Motorcycles.* New York: Roy Publishers, 1962.

Caunter, Cyril Francis. *The History and Development of Cycles.* London: H.M. Stationery Office, 1955-58.

Clifford, Peter A. *History of the Tour of Britain.* London: International Cyclists Saddle Club, 1967.

Cuthbertson, Tom. *Anybody's Bike Book.* Berkeley, California: Ten Speed Press, 1971.

Cycling Book of Maintenance, 5th Edition. London: Temple Press Books, 1961.

English, Ronald. *Adventure Cycling.* London: N. Kaye, 1959.

———. *Cycling for You.* London: Clutterworth Press, 1964.

Frankel, Godfrey. *Bike-ways.* New York: Sterling Publishing Company, 1950.

Frankel, Godfrey and Lillian. *101 Things to Do With a Bike.* New York: Sterling Publishing Company, 1961; rev. ed., 1968.

Frood-Barclay, Robin. *Tackle Cycle Sport This Way.* London: S. Paul, 1962.

Henderson, Noel Gordon. *Continental Cycle Racing.* London: Pelham Books, 1970.

Houston, Jack. *Wandering Wheels.* Grand Rapids, Michigan: Baker Book House, 1970.

How to Improve Your Cycling. New Rochelle, New York: Soccer.

Kraynick, Steve. *Bicycle Owner's Complete Handbook.* Los Angeles: Floyd Clymer Publications, 1960.

———. *Your Bicycle.* Peoria, Illinois: Manual Arts Press, 1948.

Leete, Harley M., ed. *The Best of Bicycling!* New York: Trident Press, 1970.

Leonard, Irving Albert. *When Bikehood Was in Flower; Sketches of Early Cycling.* South Tamworth, New Hampshire: Bearcamp Press, 1969.

Macfarlan, Allan A. *Boy's Book of Biking.* New York: Washington Square Press, 1970.

McGonagle, Seamus. *The Bicycle in Love, Life, War, and Literature.* London: Pelham Books, 1968.

Messenger, Charles. *Conquer the World.* London: Pelham Books, 1968.

———. *Cycling Crazy.* London: Pelham Books, 1970.

Moore, Harold. *The Complete Cyclist.* London: Sir Isaac Pitman & Sons, 1935, and New York: Pitman Publishing Co., 1960.

Murphy, Dervla. *Full Tilt.* New York: Dutton, 1965.

Nelson, Janet. *Biking for Fun and Fitness.* New York: Award Books, 1970.

Palmer, Arthur Judson. *Riding High.* New York: Dutton, 1956.

Pullen, A.L. *Cycling Handbook.* London: Sir Isaac Pitman & Sons, 1960.

Shaw, Reginald Cairns. *Teach Yourself Cycling.* London: English Universities Press, 1967.

———. *This Great Club of Ours: The Story of the Cyclists' Touring Club.* London: The Cyclists' Touring Club, 1953.

Sloane, Eugene, A. *The Complete Book of Bicycling.* New York: Trident Press, 1970.

Sumner, Philip Lawton. *Early Bicycles.* London: Evelyn, 1966.

Taylor, Marshall W. *The Fastest Bicycle Rider in the World.* Worcester, Massachusetts: Wormley Publishing Co., 1928.

Ward, Peter. *King of Sports.* 1967.

Way, Robert. *Cycling Manual.* London: Temple Press Books, 1967.

Williamson, Geoffrey. *Wheels Within Wheels.* London: Geoffrey Bles, Ltd., 1966.

Woodforde, John. *The Story of the Bicycle.* New York: Universe Books, 1971.

Chart 1				PRINCIPAL TYPES OF GEARS

Chart 1 PRINCIPAL TYPES OF GEARS

Type of Hub	No. of Speeds	Advantages	Disadvantages
No gears; brake by stopping pedals.	1	Very low cost and great simplicity.	Pedals rotate continually.
No gears; coaster brakes.	1	Low cost and relative simplicity. Brakes provide safety.	Limited hill-climbing ability.
Pedal-operated epicyclic gears; pedal-operated coaster brakes.	2	Simple, nearly maintenance free. Rider can keep both hands free to steer. Good for pre-teen riders. Good hill-climbing ability.	Limited high-speed performance (no low pedal-to-wheel ratio).
Lever-operated epicyclic gears; pedal-operated coaster brakes.	3	Easy pedalling both on hills and at high speed. Rider can keep both hands free to steer except when changing gears.	Hand-operated gear change may be difficult for youngsters.
Lever-operated epicyclic gears; caliper brakes.	3	Simpler hub than 3-speed with coaster brakes. Freewheel effect when back-pedalling is convenient when positioning pedals.	Hand-operated brakes and gears may be difficult for youngsters.
Derailleur gears; caliper brakes.	5, 10, or 15	Wide range of pedal-to-wheel ratios allows easy pedalling under most road conditions.	Gear-changing procedure may be complicated for youngsters to learn. Mechanism is more prone to damage or maladjustment.

Chart 2 COMMON ACCESSORIES

For Safety	For Convenience	For Comfort
Lock (built-in, long shank padlock, chain, cable)	Speedometer	Bike radio
Bike tools	Mileage meter (cyclometer)	Special seat or saddle
Bell	Kickstand	Handlebar grips
Horn (electric or squeeze bulb)	Basket (wire or woven, front or rear mounting)	Handlebar tape
Battery-operated headlight (removable or fixed)	Pannier bags	Refreshment bottle & cage (frame or handlebar mount)
All-in-one generator headlight	Touring bags	Bicycle riding gloves
Generator light set	Lock and tool bag	Cycling clothes
Taillight	Luggage rack	Windshield
Directional lights	Luggage straps	
Reflectors (front, rear, and side)	Baby seat	
Reflector pedals	Quick-release wheel hub skewers	
Reflective safety tape	Bike storage hook set	
Handlebar plugs	Automobile bike-carrying rack (cartop or rear-lid)	
Rear-view mirror	Bicycling shoes	
Air pump (foot or frame)	Trailer for excess baggage	
Chainguard	Toe clips and straps	
Crash helmet		

Chart 3

THE RIGHT FRAME SIZE
(Using Rider's Leg Length)

Leg Length	Wheel Size	Frame Size	Typical Top Tube-to-Ground Distance	Typical Minimum Saddle-to-Ground Distance
15″	12″	8″	16″	17½″
19″	16″	10″	20″	21″
23″	20″	13″	23½″	24″
23½″	20″	14″	24″	25″
24″	20″	15″	25″	27″
26″	24″	16″	27″	29½″
29″	26″	18″	30″	32″
29½″	26″	21″	30″	33″
30″	26″	22″	30½″	34½″
31″	27″	22″	31½″	35½″
32½″	27″	24″	33″	37″

NOTE: (1) Not all leg lengths or wheel size/frame size combinations are shown here—just a representative sample. If your leg measurement isn't shown here, use the one that's nearest. Or, if your measurement is halfway between two listed lengths, use the smaller of the two.

(2) Top tube-to-ground distance and minimum saddle-to-ground distance for a given wheel size/frame size combination can vary slightly from model to model. If in doubt, measure the bicycle you're interested in. Top tube-to-ground distance should be about one inch longer than leg length.

Chart 4   ## THE RIGHT FRAME SIZE (Using rider's height)

Rider Height	Frame Size
Under 5′0″	19″ or smaller
5′1″ to 5′9″	21″ or 22″
5′10″ to 6′0″	23″ or 24″
6′1″ and up	24″ or larger

Chart 5   ## RECOMMENDED TIRE PRESSURES

Tire Size (Inches)	Air Pressure (Pounds/square inch)
12 X all casing sizes	35
16 X all casing sizes	40
18 X all casing sizes	45
20 X 1⅜	55
20 X 1¾	40
20 X 2⅛	35
24 X 1⅜	55
24 X 1¾	40
24 X 2⅛	35
26 X 1¼ or 1⅜	55
26 X 1¾	40
26 X 2⅛	35
27 X 1¼	70
27-inch sewn tubular touring tires	85 to 100 (rear) 75 to 90 (front)

Chart 6   ## POSSIBLE LUGGAGE FOR A TOURING TRIP

Equipment	Clothing
Repair kit, spare tube and chain links	Lightweight windbreaker
Tire pump	Long-sleeved shirt for sunburn protection
Knife	Short-sleeved shirt
Flashlight	Slacks
First aid kit	Shorts
Cooking & eating equipment	Cap or other head covering
Sleeping bag and/or tent	Wool socks
Maps and a compass	Extra underwear
Mosquito and sunburn lotion	Rain cape or jacket
Pencil and paper	Comfortable riding shoes
Sunglasses	

Chart 7   **BIKE PARTS PRICES – Early 1972**   **Chart 8**   **TYPICAL BIKE PRICES**

Frame (adult lightweight, typical U.S. brand)	$14.00
Gooseneck (handlebar stem)	$2.25 to 5.75
Handlebars	$2.00 to 4.50
Handlebar grips	$0.50 to 1.00
Pedals (pair)	$1.50 to 4.50
Chain (complete with master link)	$1.50 to 3.50
Tires (pair, clincher type)	$7.00 to 9.00
Tubes (pair)	$3.00 to 4.00
Front wheel (without tire or tube, 26"X1⅜")	$6.50 to 12.50
Coaster brake rear wheel (without tire or tube, 26"X1⅜")	$12.50 to 16.25
Saddle	$2.50 to 10.00
Fork	$6.95 to 11.50
Crank bearing set (complete less crank)	$2.00 to 5.00
Crank (set)	$7.00 and up
Fenders (pair, with braces)	$3.75 to 5.50
Fender braces (each)	$0.35
Spokes (each)	$0.10
Kickstand	$1.25 to 2.50
Front wheel cone	$0.20 to 0.50
Front axle	$0.25 to 0.50
Rear axle	$1.50
Ball bearings (one packet)	$0.50
Brake cable	$1.25 to 1.60
Rear derailleur mechanism (Campagnolo Record)	$27.55
Rear derailleur mechanism (Simplex Prestige)	$6.50
Front derailleur mechanism (Campagnolo Record)	$13.50
Front derailleur mechanism (Simplex Prestige)	$5.25
Headset (complete, typical U.S. brands)	$1.50 to 3.50
Headset (complete, Campagnolo Record)	$14.25

Type of Bike	Price
Small beginner's bike, bargain-priced	$30
Small beginner's bike, top quality	$52
High-rise, 1-speed, bargain-priced	$40
High-rise, 5-speed, top quality	$92
Touring model, 3-speed, medium quality	$50
Touring model, 3-speed, top quality	$87
10-speed lightweight, bargain-priced	$65
10-speed lightweight, medium quality	$120
10-speed lightweight, professional's choice	$350
Custom-built 10-speed	$400 plus
Professional track bike	$227
Tandem, 1-speed	$114
Tandem, 5-speed	$145
Unicycle	$42
Adult three-wheeler, 3-speed, high quality	$164

INDEX

Page numbers in bold face indicate illustrations.